ZAMORA
CHANGE AND CONTINUITY IN A MEXICAN TOWN

ORIOL PI-SUNYER

CASE STUDIES IN

CULTURAL ANTHROPOLOGY

GENERAL EDITORS

George and Louise Spindler

STANFORD UNIVERSITY

ZAMORA

*Change and Continuity
in a Mexican Town*

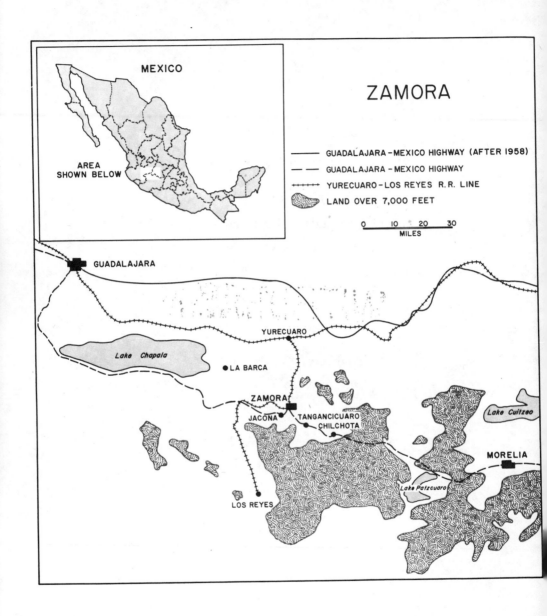

MEXICO

AREA
SHOWN BELOW

ZAMORA

— GUADALAJARA–MEXICO HIGHWAY (AFTER 1958)
— — GUADALAJARA–MEXICO HIGHWAY
+++ YURECUARO–LOS REYES R.R. LINE
LAND OVER 7,000 FEET

0   10   20   30
MILES

GUADALAJARA

YURECUARO

Lake Chapala

LA BARCA

ZAMORA

JACONA   TANGANCICUARO
CHILCHOTA

Lake Cuitzeo

MORELIA

Lake Patzcuaro

LOS REYES

ZAMORA

Change and Continuity
in a Mexican Town

By
ORIOL PI-SUNYER
University of Massachusetts

HOLT, RINEHART AND WINSTON, INC.

NEW YORK   CHICAGO   SAN FRANCISCO   ATLANTA
DALLAS   MONTREAL   TORONTO   LONDON   SYDNEY

To Polly

Library of Congress Cataloging in Publication Data

Pi-Sunyer, Oriol.
Zamora: change and continuity in a Mexican town.
(Case studies in cultural anthropology)

Bibliography: p. 114
1. Zamora, Mexico—Social conditions. 2. Zamora, Mexico—Social
life and customs. 3. Zamora, Mexico—Economic conditions.
I. Title. II. Series
HN120.Z3P5   301.29'72'3   73–2369
ISBN: 0–03–085769–4

Foreword

About the Series

These case studies in cultural anthropology are designed to bring to students, in beginning and intermediate courses in the social sciences, insights into the richness and complexity of human life as it is lived in different ways and in different places. They are written by men and women who have lived in the societies they write about and who are professionally trained as observers and interpreters of human behavior. The authors are also teachers, and in writing their books they have kept the students who will read them foremost in their minds. It is our belief that when an understanding of ways of life very different from one's own is gained, abstractions and generalizations about social structure, cultural values, subsistence techniques, and the other universal categories of human social behavior become meaningful.

About the Author

Oriol Pi-Sunyer was born in Barcelona, Spain. In 1939 he moved with his parents to England where he attended secondary schools and later studied at the University of London. In 1951 he went to Mexico to study anthropology at the Escuela Nacional de Anthropología and Mexico City College (now University of the Americas). He received his doctorate from Harvard University. For the past twelve years he has taught at Canadian and American universities and is currently Associate Professor of Anthropology at the University of Massachusetts, Amherst. In addition to research in Mexico, he has done field work in Guatemala, Venezuela, and Spain. He is the author of various articles and monographs dealing with ethnographic, ethnohistorical, and developmental themes and is the coauthor with Thomas R. De Gregori, an economist, of *Economic Development: The Cultural Context*. He has recently returned from Spain where he studied social conflict in a fishing community and also directed the University of Massachusetts Field Training Program in Complex Societies. He is a fellow of the American Anthropological Association and has served as consultant to several foundations and educational organizations including the Ford Foundation, Education and World Affairs, and the Institute for International Education.

About the Book

Most of the communities which anthropologists study, such as the tribe and village, are small, sometimes numbering not more than fifty to one hundred people, sometimes several thousand, but rarely more than that. Often in the past these small communities have been studied in isolation from their surrounding sociocultural, economic, and political environment. The dominance of the small isolated community in anthropological observation and conceptualization is understandable, given anthropological concerns with nonwestern, nonliterate, and technologically primitive peoples.

Recently, however, anthropology has begun to probe a larger and more complex arena. There have been studies of segments of larger communities, urbanizing communities of middling size, institutions, such as schools, as cultural subsystems, studies of whole regions, and studies of towns and small cities. The Case Studies in Cultural Anthropology include representations of all of these categories, but Oriol Pi-Sunyer's study of Zamora falls into the latter category.

Zamora is located in the northwest section of the state of Michoacán in west-central Mexico and is the largest community on the Guadalajara-Mexico City highway between Guadalajara and the Michoacán State Capital of Morelia. When the author first studied Zamora, it had a population of around 35,000. When he revisited it in 1971, there was a population of 50,819. This case study centers on this town, but within the context of the municipal unit, the *municipio*, of which Zamora is the administrative center or *cabecera*.

This case study is particularly valuable because it not only deals with a large population aggregate in a yet larger geographical-cultural region, but it also deals with two time planes. Pi-Sunyer did his first work in Zamora in 1957 and 1958 and he describes the structure of Zamora society, interpersonal and intersexual relations, and the economy for that period. Here we can see the culture, social structure, and economy of a central Mexican town before the most dramatic impact of industrialization and the American influence from the north had taken place. His description and analysis of Zamora at this period sets the stage perfectly for his last chapter written on the basis of his return visit in 1971. Here it is apparent that much of the old has remained and that many of the apparently dramatic changes are rather superficial. The lack of major structural changes in the social order raises questions as to the future. Professor Pi-Sunyer ends his case study with some fundamental questions, "Must the poor always remain dependent and subordinate? Are concepts of modernization and progress applicable only to the well-to-do sectors of society?" He points out that these are questions that face developing countries in many parts of the globe. Particularly in Latin America, modernization has done little to change the conditions of the poor.

George and Louise Spindler
General Editors

Stanford University
1973

Preface

The research upon which this case study is based was conducted during the years 1957–1958 and the summer of 1971. I originally went to Zamora as a Research Associate of M.I.T. with a grant from that institution to study a Mexican regional economy. The orientation of my research reflected the needs of the project, but I approached economic factors as an anthropologist, that is to say, in the total social and cultural context. Also, I believed then, as I continue to believe today, that in the anthropology of complex societies it is necessary to take into account the overall national culture and make as much use as possible of historical information.

The present monograph is something more than an ethnography of a Mexican town. The social structure of the town can in part be approached as a study in the exercise of economic and social power, but in order to understand Zamora, it is necessary to have some knowledge of local and national history. An ethnography of Zamora could be written in the "ethnographic present" (the period the investigator was in the field), but only at the cost of substantial distortion. Zamora is not a static entity, it has witnessed numerous changes in the lifetime of many of its inhabitants, and changes are taking place today. For these reasons I have not hesitated to look back in time and attempt to follow the major transformations which have occurred in Zamora since its foundation.

Zamora began in the sixteenth century as a settlement of Spanish colonists. The imprint of these early *zamoranos* is evident today and was felt even more strongly a dozen years ago. Codes of behavior, attitudes, and values always owe much to the past and perhaps can only be fully understood with reference to it, for in the last analysis they are customary usages transmitted from one generation to the next. Things change, new threads are woven into the cultural pattern, old practices disappear, but always a part of the past remains in the present.

It is worth noting also that Zamora has, from its earliest years, been a component of a larger whole, whether colonial New Spain, newly independent Mexico, or the contemporary Mexican Republic. For a town integrated into a national system, acculturation models are not very useful. Of course, Zamora has had to adjust to a whole series of external influences and the outside world impinges on the community, but this is a normal process of transformation, not the impact of ill-understood alien forces. The town changes as the country changes, not as rapidly or as totally as the national capital or the major cities, but steadily and appreciably.

Newcomers to Zamora, and there are many now resident in the *municipio*, complain that the town is "provincial" and its inhabitants "old-fashioned." Yet, the changes that have taken place in the last dozen years have transformed an essentially rural region into a protoindustrial one with a labor force that is increasingly dependent on factory employment. A new middle class of managers, technicians, and businessmen is developing in Zamora and may soon challenge established elites for local political, social, and economic leadership. This process of displacement has historical antecedents, for the established elites were the new power seekers only a couple of generations ago. The *mestizo* peasants, not to mention the Tarascan Indians marginal to the *municipio*, are only peripherally involved in these changes: for them, it is mostly a case of new bosses. Faces and individuals change; demands remain much the same.

I have done my best to present a fair picture of Zamora. Some of the citizens of Zamora read portions of an earlier monograph (Pi-Sunyer 1967). They tell me that they found it interesting and at times even amusing, amusing in the sense that they played a "who is he writing about now" type of game. Although I pulled no anthropological punches—I had written of economic control, social dominance, and other potentially touchy subjects—I was received on my return with great courtesy and a willingness to help in the furtherance of my researches. My first debt, therefore, is to the people of Zamora.

I have not given the town a fictional name. It is difficult to do so for a community of this size, the second largest town in the State of Michoacán. However, to assure some privacy, informants remain nameless. By this expedient, I hope, the dictates of anonymity are sufficiently served.

Zamora was my first major anthropological venture. I went into the field with my wife, then also a graduate student in anthropology. The "we" in the text should be read as more than a stylistic device. Polly was not simply "the wife of the anthropologist"—important though that was for my morale and general well-being—but a co-worker and an excellent participant in and observer of the local scene. In substantial part, this is also her book.

Of colleagues and teachers, there are many that warrant thanks. I will limit myself to those whose help was most instrumental in the realization of the original research. First and foremost, I wish to take this opportunity to record my most sincere appreciation for all the help and guidance given to me by the late Clyde Kluckhohn. It was he who insisted that an ethnographer should look not only at the present, but also to the past; not only at the community, but to its place in the total national culture. Cora DuBois, Evon Z. Vogt, and Gordon Willey were unstinting in their time and counsel and did much to smooth the path of a neophyte anthropologist. It was Everett E. Hagen of the M.I.T. Center for International Studies who procured the funds to send me to the field. He believed that there was common ground that should be explored between anthropology and economics. In the last analysis, without his help neither this book nor the original report could have been realized. Finally, my thanks go to Robert Wauchope of the Middle American Research Institute of Tulane University for permission to use material originally published in the Reports of the Middle American Research Institute.

Closer to home, I wish to thank Mrs. J. W. Fair of Amherst, Massachusetts. She found time in her own busy schedule to type the manuscript of this study, but more than this, her years of experience were placed at my disposal with the result that orthography, punctuation, and style were much improved between rough draft and finished product.

Most of the material for this report is derived from field work conducted during

1957 and 1958. However, since I have not limited myself to these years and, in fact, have purposely tried to trace a historical progression, as well as place Zamora in the context of a broader national culture, the reader might benefit from keeping in mind the following spatial and temporal frames:

Chapter 1 is an outline of Mexican colonial history with emphasis on the cultural attributes which Spanish *conquistadores* and settlers brought with them to the New World. Chapter 2 is a general introduction to the town and the region with some observations on the changes which have occurred between 1958 and 1971. Chapters 3–8 consider various aspects of the society and culture of the *municipio*. The temporal frame of these chapters is the Zamora of a dozen years ago, thus providing a base line for a discussion in Chapter 9 of the major changes and discontinuities which I observed on my return to Zamora in 1971.

O. P.-Ş.

Amherst, Mass.
January 1973

Contents

1 / Historical perspective

ORIGINS

The countries of Latin America, with the exception of Haiti and Brazil, owe their origins as modern states to successful wars of independence which liberated them from the political control of Spain. However, the Spanish colonial experience was of such duration, the cultural influences so deep, that the core of the national cultures of these republics may still be recognized as of distinctly Spanish origin. This common heritage is recognized not only by outside observers, but is no less a reality for many of the citizens of the nations in question. Those who give thought to such matters define their countries as *naciones hispano-americanas* (Hispanic-American countries) and the lands south of the Rio Grande as *Ibero-américa*. Shared historical experience, a common European heritage, and similar social and economic problems, all contribute to a great deal that is alike in the nations of Hispanic-America. Much of this similarity, though, tends to be restricted to the "national" elements, while the specific cultural composition of the different Republics presents a picture of considerable diversity.

What we have in Hispanic-America—and to some extent this holds true for Latin America as a whole—is cultural variety within a certain framework of unity. In recent years various efforts have been directed as isolating and classifying culturally meaningful units and groupings. Some students have worked on a broad continental canvas, others have investigated the composition of national cultures, while still others have directed their attention at subcultural entities, variously referred to as "culture types" (Steward 1958: 64ff.), "orders" (Redfield 1957: 21ff), "typologies" (Wagley and Harris 1955), "components" (Adams 1956), and "multiple societies" (Nash 1957).

These units within nation and region vary in size and composition. They range from the closed corporate societies of indigenous communities, largely marginal to the national cultures and the general ethos of national life, to cosmopolitan culture components the basic heritage of which is European and whose members typically fill positions of prestige and authority in their respective lands. It is clear that while some of these units represent distinctions within nations and regions, others are not limited to nation and locality, but rather are elements with cross-cultural and cross-national validity. This is largely true of Latin American elites, and as the research of the late Oscar Lewis indicates (Lewis 1959; 1961; 1966;

1

1970) a similar case can be made for a "culture of poverty" whose chief locus is the burgeoning urban centers of Latin America.

Contemporary Mexico has been described as "multiple society" (Nash 1957: 825) and as a representative of "Mestizo America" (Gillin 1949), by which it is understood that the Republic harbors within its borders indigenous communities which continue to operate outside the mainstream of the national culture.

It is critically important to understand what this entails in cultural, political, and racial terms. Legally, there is but one category of citizen in Mexico, and the law recognizes no difference between an Otomí shepherd boy, a Tarascan peasant, and the president of Mexico: all are Mexican and theoretically have the same rights and obligations of citizenship. Culturally, the distinction is generally made between Indian and non-Indian, the latter typically referred to in the literature as *mestizo*. It would be wrong, though, to see this as primarily a racial distinction. In Mexico a racial synthesis has been going on for more than four centuries and today few inhabitants, regardless of cultural orientation or social position, are without some degree of Indian genetic admixture.

This genetic fusion, however, has been paralleled only partially by cultural admixture. Some Indian elements, it is true, have penetrated the national culture, mostly in the form of words, food habits, crops, and some material traits. Nevertheless, cultural loans have been remarkably one-sided. Historically, the process has been one of gradual assimilation of the Indian population into the cultural ways of a European-derived dominant society.

This dominant society or national culture—many members of which are in fact socially and economically subordinate—is "national" in the sense that its members respond to institutions at least in part structured at the national level and share a body of values and behavior that are national in scope. Individuals identify as *mexicanos* (Mexicans) and recognize an affinity with other Mexicans. In contrast, Indian identity is essentially local or communal.

Inherited racial characteristics are in themselves very secondary, what matters is cultural symbolism. Regardless of racial composition, if a person lives as a Mexican, he is so regarded. Outstanding differences which are recognized as distinguishing Indians from *mexicanos* are those of language, dress, and tribal or communal affiliation. Explicit recognition of this situation is encountered among both *mexicanos* and Indians. Given the fact that differences between the two groups are defined largely in terms of cultural attributes, it is possible for an Indian to move from Indian status to one of acceptance by *mexicanos*. This step is in fact taking place all the time, usually at the lower levels of national society.

While it is valid to speak of a Mexican national culture, this in turn is made up of a variety of subcultures. Subcultural differences, as in any complex society, cut along a variety of planes, such as class, region, and community. There are urban and rural subcultures, as well as elite and lower-class subcultures. However, seen as a whole, the national culture of Mexico is clearly recognized as a variety of that macro-entity sometimes referred to as Western civilization. Many of the components that make up Mexican national culture are akin to those found in other Western countries. For the reader this may have the advantage of some familiarity, perhaps at the expense of the exotic elements that one may come to associate with anthropological monographs. Mexicans speak Spanish, are at least nominal Catholics, subscribe to a republican form of government, are guided by a Latin-type legal system, wear European style clothes, drink such familiar beverages as beer and Coca-Cola, and when able to afford it, are as eager to acquire cars and appliances as mainstream North Americans.

However, the mere identification of shared elements may in fact tend to emphasize similarities at the expense of those differences which give Mexican national culture its distinctive coloration. A Mexican community is much more than Middletown in the tropics, and more than the sum of Spanish colonial experience. A further, and vitally important, point is that the culture of colonial Mexico cannot be viewed as a carbon copy of sixteenth-century Spanish culture. As George Foster (1960: 227) has pointed out, the colonial process inevitably entails selection and reinterpretation of traits from the donor culture.

THE COLONIAL ROOTS OF MEXICAN CULTURE

The original Spanish settlers of Mexico, the men of the conquest, brought with them the patterns of the landed nobility of Castile and those parts of Spain annexed to the kingdom in the course of the *reconquista*, the reconquest of Spain from the Moors. These colonist-conquerors represented the first generation of Castilians to come of age after the period of the long Moorish wars had terminated with the taking of the last Islamic stronghold of Granada in 1492. It is important to note that Mexico, subdued within a few years of the fall of Tenochtitlán, the Aztec capital, in 1521, was the first mainland territory to be incorporated into the Spanish crown. The temporal relation between *reconquista* and conquest was therefore stronger in the case of Mexico, or New Spain as it was soon called, than in other New World dominions. In the latter part of the sixteenth century, and increasingly so throughout the colonial period, settlers and adventurers crossed the Atlantic from other parts of Spain. But the first years were of crucial importance. As George Foster (1960: 232) has noted, "The basic outlines of the new colonial cultures took place at a rapid rate. Once they became comparatively well integrated and offered preliminary answers to the most pressing problems of the settlers, their forms became more rigid; they may be said to have crystallized."

For the most part the *conquistadores* represent a type that evolved as a product of the *reconquista*: the *hidalgos*. Typically, the *hidalgo* was a Catholic and a royalist, a man who had never worked with his hands, and abhorred trade and industry. He had been educated to a tradition where military prowess brought rewards in land, slaves, and titles. As long as there was land to conquer and wars to fight, his services remained in demand, but with the end of the Moorish conflict it appeared that the *hidalgos* had fought themselves out of a significant role in the political and military life of the nation.

Born too late, or in some cases not lucky enough, to share in the distribution of the last of the Moorish territories, many made their way to the recently discovered Antilles. Here, though, conditions were far from ideal. The Indians inhabiting the islands were poor marginal agriculturalists little able to produce a surplus for the new invaders. A certain amount of gold was extracted, but this at the expense of so many Indian lives that in a few years insufficient natives survived to provide for the food needs of the Spaniards. The Spanish colonist, greatly averse to working the land—it was not for this that he had crossed the Atlantic—was in many cases faced with starvation. In short, the Antilles failed to provide those opportunities for rapid wealth and military distinction so desired by the Spanish immigrant of the times.

It was from bases in the West Indies that Spaniards first set out to explore, and if possible conquer, the American mainland. The tale of the conquest of Mexico, a theme for historical works and popular literature, has become a familiar epic of the destruction of an ancient civilization by a small band of resolute men. All that need concern us here is that in no way, except in the greatness of the prize, was this adventure very different from the many Spanish New World campaigns of the early years of the sixteenth century.

After Cortés and his soldiers had defeated the Aztec forces, the conquerors set about to establish a society modelled as closely on that of their homeland as opportunity and the local situation permitted. The *conquistadores*, of course, had to contend with factors that limited their field of action. The church and the crown had their own plans for overseas territories and much of the formal political and religious organization was imposed by royal decree and ecclesiastical ordinance. But for a long time the ideal of the dominant sectors of society remained those of the soldier-landlord, and many of the cultural patterns and values still observable in contemporary Mexican national culture must be traced to these Spanish cultural antecedents.

Colonial society in Mexico, especially in the early periods, was basically a two-class, or perhaps more correctly, two-caste, system with a small propertied group, mainly landholders, controlling the bulk of the resources of the country. The pattern seems to have been that typical of traditionally oriented colonial settler societies: an educated landholding elite monopolizing the bulk of the positions of power (social, economic, religious, and political) not in the hands of homeland appointees. This situation would be especially applicable to the early formative years following conquest and primary consolidation.

Very early in colonial history the elite splits into two interest groups: the Spaniards, or *peninsulares*, and the *criollos*, the American-born creole aristocracy. This never represented a basic division in attitudes and values, but rather should be regarded as two groups competing for positions of control. Although the Spanish government generally favored the Spanish-born for high office, the resentment of the *criollos* cannot be construed as a popular or democratic movement to overthrow the despotic rule of the rich and powerful. When independence was won, the social structure of the country changed but little and this helps to explain much of the continuity of social and cultural patterns into the post-independence period.

Not all Spaniards and *criollos* were necessarily rich, not all owned vast land-holdings. But so strong was the mystique of the *conquistadores* that a feeling of aristocratic privilege seems to have permeated everyone with a white skin. Apparently, the poor Spaniard on landing in the New World refused to practice a trade, if he had one, or work the land for hire, considering such activities fit only for Negroes and Indians. What we have in colonial Mexico is a situation in which all segments of the intrusive culture share a similar set of attitudes regarding not only what may be termed the good life, but in fact the only possible, the only respectable, life under colonial conditions.

Obviously, these ideals are of a type that while they may be universally aspired to cannot always be universally achieved. But to a substantial degree they were in Mexico. In natural resources Mexico was infinitely richer than Castile. Over and above this it offered the colonist an indispensable prerequisite for success: manpower. Land, minerals, and, after the initial bloodletting of the conquest, a docile population of agriculturally trained Indians made up the necessary equation for individual fortune. But without doubt the most important factor was population. For the *conquistador* it was not the man that made the land, but rather it was the fruits of the land extracted by someone else that made the man. "Work," as the Spanish philosopher Ortega y Gasset (1948: 118–119) writes commenting on this type of society, "is not therefore a means to just gain, but rather a condition. The noble, the magistrate, the ecclesiastical dignitary, have the obligation to provide their conduct with the pomp and ostentation which correspond to their function and hierarchical position."

Although the official policies of government and church influenced the behavior of Spanish settlers in that restrictions were placed on the all-out exploitation of the indigenous population, it was nevertheless the Indian rather than the Spaniard who was forced to make major adjustments. The Spaniard came to Mexico with the blithe assurance of cultural and religious superiority. It is true that individual Spaniards—some of them men of great moral authority—decried the treatment accorded to the Indians, and that scholars of integrity and insight have left for us valuable descriptions of Aztec and Maya society, but, nevertheless, the attitude of the average colonist was essentially exploitative.

Faced with this situation, the Indian managed as best he could. Some avenues of escape remained partially open. Spacially, the Indian might head for the hills to evade Spanish control and "reduction" into Spanish supervised settlements, the "strategic hamlets" of the times; culturally he could cultivate patterns of passive resistance. But the capacity of these channels were obviously limited and for the most part it was a case of adjust or perish.

In order to understand colonial Mexico we should keep in mind that within a few years of the conquest aboriginal society was deprived of its indigenous leadership. Indian elites were either killed in the initial battles, co-opted into the Spanish ruling class (and hence ceased to be Indians in a cultural sense), or lost their elite status and were merged with the peasantry. At one stroke, Indian society was reduced to a truncated social order devoid of any element capable of organized resistance. Soon, there evolved a caste-like relationship between Spaniards and Indians structured on the basis of patronage. This system rigidly defined the forms of subordination and superordination in interpersonal relations.

With regard to the crown, and by extension, to all civil authority, the Spanish settler modelled his behavior in a manner designed to duplicate the feudal situation traditional to his homeland. The soldier who had fought in the New World (or a man whose ancestor had done so) felt no qualms about directing personal correspondence to the king in Spain, especially should he judge himself unfairly treated by some subordinate official. One of the most jealously guarded rights of the Castilian noble was that of personal audience with the sovereign. To be denied this privilege was almost equivalent to a loss of noble standing.

Naturally, it was difficult for the majority of Spaniards in Mexico to exercise this privilege. Still, not a few men, including Cortés himself, made the long trip to court in order to plead their cases. Others, of whom the best known is perhaps Bernal Díaz del Castillo, one of the chief chroniclers of the conquest, had to be satisfied with a letter in place of a personal audience.

This right of appeal, this insistence on being heard, is but one facet of a phenomenon that has long interested students of Spanish and Latin American culture, namely "individualism." Individualism obviously means different things to different people. For the Spaniard the core concept was an ideal of personal absolutism, the notion that every man is an independent personality with a right to honorable treatment. It can show itself in a general disdain for the formal channels of government and it no doubt helps account for the aloofness and personal dignity that have often been described as part of the Spanish character.

These traits are not unrelated to early colonial history. The chroniclers themselves insist that a major motivation for the enterprise of the Indies was a quest for honor, honor that could best be achieved by the ennobling experience of battle. It is worth noting that at the very genesis of New Spain, Hernán Cortés mounted his expedition in open defiance of Diego Velasquez, Governor of Cuba. The conquest of Mexico was therefore not the work of some representative of the crown, but a strictly private undertaking without financial or other support from the state. It is true that Mexico was subdued "in the name" of the Emperor Charles V, but this was the standard procedure in conquest and exploration, and it should not be thought of as an abdication of their rights by *conquistadores.*

One may wonder why given the propensity for individual action and the disdain for authority on the part of *conquistadores,* colonial Mexican history is marked by stability rather than conflict. Part of the answer is that early colonial history coincided with a period of very strong royal control and the establishment of a tradition of royal absolutism. Charles V and Phillip II were not men likely to tolerate any move contrary to their royal will. They showed this clearly with regard to their European possessions, and it is evident that if these monarchs were able to cope with insurrections in some of their populous and well-organized European principalities, no handful of men in America could hope to set themselves up in opposition to the power of the crown.

Spanish settlement in Mexico, especially in the early years, suffered from the type of demographic imbalance common to many expeditions of a largely military nature. Those who crossed the Atlantic to make their fortunes in the New World generally sailed without the encumbrance of wives and family. No doubt this was in part due to selective factors in favor of the most mobile elements of the population, the single men. Also, one should remember the logistic problems inherent in supplying overseas expeditions in the early sixteenth century. Even thirty years after the conquest not more than a few thousand Spaniards were settled in Mexico, while in the years immediately following the fall of the Aztec Empire the number of Spaniards should be reckoned in hundreds rather than in thousands.

In those early years, Indian revolt and Negro insurrection were regarded as very real dangers and it was thus held imperative that every cargo landing on Mexican shores contribute something to the military strength of the colony. The problem was one of priorities. Men capable of bearing arms were naturally the most valued commodities; women, on the otherhand, hardly added much to the military posture. For other—that is to say sexual—purposes there was a plentiful supply of Indian women. From the very first, Spaniards were in no way averse to establishing unions with Indian females. There were certainly no fears regarding the impropriety of sexual relations with members of a different race, such as have at times been expressed (but seldom manifested in actual behavior) by other European groups.

As we have noted, though, the Indian was assigned a position of social inferiority in the framework of colonial society. Patterns of male dominance and female subordination were thus in part grounded on a kind of double conquest. But a situation of female subordination is not something that simply evolved from a conquest culture. Patterns of male dominance, a double standard of sexual behavior, and close chaperonage and seclusion of female members of the family are all demonstrable in sixteenth-century Spain and, in fact, probably represent a broad Mediterranean culture pattern still evident today.

2 / The town and the region

THE SETTING

The town of Zamora is located in the northwest section of the state of Michoacán, west-central Mexico. The name of the town is also applied to the *municipio*, the municipal unit of which Zamora is the administrative center or *cabecera*. In order to avoid confusion, "Zamora" will refer to the town proper, and the *municipio* will be identified as "the *municipio* of Zamora," or, more simply, "the *municipio*."

As *cabecera*, Zamora administers and controls twenty-six small neighboring communities the largest of which has some 3000 inhabitants. In 1958 Zamora had a population of under 35,000 while the *municipio* total came to around 46,000. By 1971 the town alone had a population of 57,819, while the population of the *municipio* had grown to 82,943.

Zamora is on the Guadalajara–Mexico City highway midway between Guadalajara and the state capital of Morelia. Along this 277-mile stretch, Zamora is by far the largest community, whether Indian or *mestizo*. Following the same highway, Mexico City lies 325 miles to the southeast.

Zamora is the focal point of the valley of Zamora, an area of almost 100 square kilometers. The valley forms the prize agricultural land of the *municipio* whose total area is 472 square kilometers.

GEOGRAPHY AND CLIMATE

The region of Michoacán embraced by the *municipio* is a densely populated area north of Tarascan Indian heartland, the Sierra de los Tarascos. This is high plateau country with elevations ranging from 7200 feet along the flanks of the Sierra to 5000 at Lake Chapala close to the city of Guadalajara. In this zone the demographic pattern is one of population concentration in a number of well-watered valleys of lacustrine origin. Of these, the valley of Zamora is one of the most favored.

Most of the lakes around Zamora have been drained, but one, Lake Camecuaro, remains a favorite spot for picnics and excursions. There are also a number of natural springs, or *ojos de agua*, which provide Zamora with most of its drinking

Timber from the highlands is often brought into town by pack horse or mule.

water. These basins and the former borders of lakes and marshes attracted Spanish settlement in colonial times. They afforded both year-round pastures for cattle and locations for irrigated wheat farms.

The natural cover of the area varies according to altitude. Oak and pine forests, now much reduced, occupy only the summits of the higher hills. The lower slopes and plains carry an association of grasses and shrubs, while gallery forests of *ahuacate* and other laurels are found in the draws within the hills and along watercourses.

Zamora itself lies 1500 meters (5000 feet) above sea level, but about half the area of the *municipio* is hill land of considerably higher elevation. The high slopes of the *municipio* are good only for rough grazing and very marginal agriculture. The hills in the immediate vicinity of the town have been bare for generations; throughout the area deforestation increases as more stands are cut to meet the construction needs of the *cabecera* and the surrounding communities. The ravages of the *carboneros*, the makers of charcoal, and those who chop wood for fuel have also taken their toll. In the town more and more households depend on electricity and butane gas for light and fuel, but poorer town families and most peasants still rely on wood or charcoal. The *municipio* faces a problem of increasing erosion, decimation of timber lands, and the silting up of irrigation channels. Nevertheless, in contrast to many other parts of Mexico, this area of Michoacán still retains a fair proportion of its natural cover.

The climate is of the type classified as *tierra templada* (temperate) in Mexico. Temperatures seldom fall below sixty degrees Fahrenheit or rise much above seventy-five degrees. Considerably colder spells do occur most winters, and since houses are not built to withstand the cold and heating is perfunctory, winters can be uncomfortable. Precipitation is seasonal, eighty percent of the annual rainfall (649.9 mm, about 25.6 inches) falling from June to September. The months immediately preceding the *lluvias*, the rainy season, are dry and relatively hot.

Rainfall plus irrigation support a flourishing agriculture in the better endowed parts of the *municipio*. The basic source of water is the Rio Duero, a stream that rises twenty-three miles southeast of Zamora in the hills of Otacuaro near the village of Carapan. During the rainy season the banks of the Duero are apt to overflow and in especially bad years the streets of Zamora may remain under two or three feet of water for as much as a week or ten days.

CULTURAL CHARACTERISTICS

Since its foundation in the second half of the sixteenth century, Zamora has retained its character as a European-derived community. Even though geographically close, Indians and Zamoranos maintain little significant contact. This is especially true of the *cabecera*, but hardly less so for the *mestizo* peasant communities which make up the rest of the *municipio*.

It is not that Indians are exactly strangers to Zamora. They are to be found in some numbers every Sunday, the chief market day, and a few Tarascans—selling garden produce on the street corners or buying necessities in town—are part of the normal street scene. However, the closeness of the Tarascan communities has not resulted in the borrowing of many elements from the indigenous society. At most, Zamora housewives will buy an occasional basket or pot, perhaps some wooden kitchen utensils, or a beaten copper pan. In the main, the boundary maintaining mechanisms of language and a dominant culture have proved more than sufficient not only to entrench *mestizo* identity, but also to reduce Indian material influences to the minimum. Indeed, the tide has run in the opposite direction: the pre-conquest Tarascan frontier was situated well to the northwest of the *municipio*, but already by the middle of the eighteenth century not only Zamora, but also much of the surrounding countryside, was predominantly spanish-speaking.

That the Zamora of today is a *mestizo* town is evident to even the most casual observer. The language is, of course, Spanish, but the surprising thing is that in 1950 not a single monolingual Indian was to be found in the whole *municipio*.[1] There were perhaps a score of individuals, mostly women, with some knowledge of Tarascan, but they also spoke Spanish and were already highly acculturated.

The dress of both men and women similarly reflect the *mestizo* orientation of the locality. Women wear dresses and blouses of European style, while most men dress in khaki pants and casual shirts. There is nothing in the costume of either men or women that distinguishes them from other Mexicans. Increasingly, the middle- and upper-class sectors of the population, especially the young, dress in

---

[1] It is interesting to note that while the 1950 census records no monolingual speakers of Indian languages, the 1970 census has 325 respondents who speak native languages. Of this total, 60 do not speak Spanish. These figures reflect the recent in-migration of peasants into the *municipio*, only a fraction of whom are Indians. As mestizoization progresses, the number of Indian speakers, both bilingual and monolingual, is bound to fall.

styles that would not be out of place in any American or European city. Today, miniskirts and pantsuits cause little comment, and for men lightweight business suits have grown in popularity over the past dozen years. On the whole, men tend to dress more casually than women who seem especially concerned in being fashionable and neatly dressed. Only the old and the poor wear clothes that may be thought of as typically Mexican: wide brimmed straw hats for the men, long cotton dresses and *rebozos*, the Mexican shawl, for the women. In 1958 a few old gentlemen still favored the riding boots and tailored pants of their youth, the kind of attire that one associates with old photographs of the Mexican Revolution. For a minority of the young, modernization involves all the material trappings of contemporary youth culture, including long hair, bellbottoms, and wire-rim glasses.

Food habits can serve as another guide of cultural affiliation. The eating of *tortillas*, the flat maize cakes of the country, is an element of Indian culture that through the centuries has been thoroughly integrated into peasant and lower-class life styles. *Tortillas* are eaten in Zamora, but much less so than wheat bread. The better restaurants automatically serve bread, usually in the form of small rolls, and more than once on asking for *tortillas* I have been told that none were available.

In Mexico wheat bread was introduced by Spanish colonists and is a characteristic of long-established *mestizo* areas and large urban centers. Heavy bread consumption is thus a good indicator of early Spanish influence. It is true that the poorer classes and the peasants of the *municipio* still rely mainly on *tortillas*, a food which they characterize as "healthier and more filling." But even here, some significant changes have taken place. Making *tortillas* is a time-consuming job involving the soaking of corn kernels in water and lime and the grinding with pestle and mortar (*mano* and *metate*) of the softened corn into a dough called *masa*. The *tortillas* must then be shaped and cooked on the griddle. Electric corn mills, where a housewife can have the corn ground for a few centavos, have been a common feature in Mexican communities for many years. Zamora has gone one step further. The town now has a plant for turning out what we might term "instant *masa*," a dehydrated corn meal which needs only water to bring to proper consistency. Naturally, the purists insists that *tortillas* made this way are not as good, but the innovation seems to have caught on. Also, machine-made *tortillas* are produced in a number of small shops.

Much besides food and clothing is referable to *mestizo* culture. The physical aspect and settlement pattern of the town closely follow the canons established for Spanish settlements in Mexico. The *cabecera* is oriented on a central plaza (Plaza de la Constitución) from which the streets radiate in more or less of a grid. This plaza is like many others in Mexico with its trees and shrubs, benches, statues of national heroes, and silver painted bandstand.

Facing the plaza are two of the most important buildings in the community, the cathedral and the *palacio municipal*, the municipal palace with local government offices, law courts, and police headquarters. Besides the cathedral, nine smaller churches and an unfinished cathedral (started early in the century) are scattered throughout the town.

Around the plaza are some of the bigger stores and the homes of the more substantial citizens. This is the "downtown" of Zamora, recognized as a privileged

The cathedral dominates the Zamora skyline.

The palacio municipal *on the central plaza houses the local government offices.*

Downtown stores with televisions, stoves, and furniture.

Typical street near town center. Houses are two-storied, tile-roofed, and mostly constructed of adobe.

area and designated by the inhabitants as *la primera cuadra*, literally the "first block," although the district encompasses substantially more than one block.

Along the periphery of the town are the houses of the very poor, the *barrios bajos* or low neighborhoods, and the new industrial plants. In 1958 efforts at building residential developments outside the traditional city limits had barely started, but the situation is very different today. There are three major *urbanizaciones* for middle- and upper-income Zamoranos, true suburbs of modern houses, but retaining the Mexican propensity for high exterior walls or enclosing fences.

It is interesting to note that this middle- and upper-class housing competes with the very low quality housing that has sprung up on the periphery of Zamora. Zamora has grown very rapidly, both as a result of a high birth rate and by in-migration, and consequently we have in a small way a phenomenon common to many Latin American urban centers, the development of shantytowns. Many of these shacks are situated on federal land along the watercourses. They are in a sense illegal constructions and the inhabitants have no security of tenure. At the same time, they don't pay any rents or taxes, but neither do they have services or utilities.

One of the strongest impressions experienced by the visitor to Zamora is that of extreme compactness of settlement. This is especially true of the older sections, but hardly less so of the new suburban developments. From the street (there is little if any sidewalk) the houses present an unbroken line, dwelling next to dwelling, which is only slightly relieved by doors and windows. The doors are nearly always closed and the windows shuttered. Most of the houses are of one or two stories. Those of the more affluent are built around a rectangular patio which is visible from the street only when the main gate is open. The houses of the poorer inhabitants often lack a central patio but instead usually have a walled backyard.

It is within the patios and the yards that much of family life takes place. Unlike the street fronts, which are seldom cared for even by those who could well afford to do so, the patios are beautiful and comfortable. The wealthier *zamoranos* decorate theirs with ornamental fountains, trees, and shady arbors, but even the poorer yards usually have a shade tree and flowering shrubs.

The majority of the houses in the *municipio* are built of adobe. As a building material, this sets certain structural limitations. Walls must be thick, doors and windows narrow, and it is virtually impossible to build adobe houses higher than two stories. Compared to concrete or fired brick, adobe is not a versatile material. It is thus understandable that architectual styles in Zamora have changed little since the Spanish first introduced the patio house plan.

The force of tradition is in many cases only slightly tempered when a change is made to other building materials. It is not unusual to find a wealthy industrialist who is building a new house of contemporary materials but in the style of a century or more ago. In part, this can be explained by the fact that the design is suited to the environment, but tradition plays its part as well. The typical Zamora house is the very antithesis of the North American suburban dwelling—no outside gardens, no lawns, no picture windows, and seldom even a new coat of paint on the exterior. The house, so to speak, faces inwards and presents a rather stark exterior to the outside world.

AGRICULTURE

The climate and soil of the *municipio* permits a wide range of crops. The region is in fact recognized as one of the garden spots of the nation, an opinion shared by both the inhabitants of the area and the less fortunate outsiders. The key to this wealth lies in the abundance of water, and in this respect the valley is by far the most favored spot. The numerous irrigation ditches running from the Duero and the Celio rivers permit the irrigation of almost all of the valley's 12,000 hectares. In this "orchard," as the Zamoranos call it, are grown abundant crops of wheat, potatoes, onions, beans, maize, tomatoes, and strawberries. In recent years the two major cash crops have been potatoes and strawberries.

Until the redistribution of land brought about by the agrarian reform program during the years 1924–1939 (in this area), the bulk of the agricultural land of the *municipio* was monopolized by a few large landowners, the *hacendados.* Prior to agrarian reform there were very few small landholders. The situation has changed radically. Most of the land—over seventy percent—is today in the hands of *ejidatarios,* peasant farmers who have been granted use-rights to small *parcelas* (allotments) of around four hectares (a little under 10 acres) of good farmland. Although the title to the land remains with the federal government, and consequently the *ejidatario* does not own the land he works, he does enjoy security of tenure and is pretty much free to do what he wishes with the land allotted to him. However, he can neither sell the land nor use it for collateral, which means that *ejido* land cannot be taken from the farmer for debts incurred. Something under thirty percent of the agricultural holdings remain in private hands, but these holdings, at least according to the letter of the law, should not exceed one hundred hectares. Many private holdings are in fact much smaller, but some individuals, as we shall see later, have managed to acquire effective control of holdings substantially larger than the legal limit. Private landowners now refer to themselves as *pequeños proprietarios,* small property owners. The term *hacendado* is now no longer used in the area.

The land of the *municipio* varies greatly in quality, much depending on the availability of water, the quality of the soil, and the gradient of the slope. The total area of the *municipio* is somewhat over 41,000 hectares and of this only some 16,000 hectares are recognized as good agricultural land. The prize lands, almost 12,000 hectares, are *tierras de riego,* irrigated lands. This is for the most part bottom lands of high quality capable of yielding two crops a year. *Tierras de humedad* are naturally wet or humid lands which while they do not make use of irrigation works are sufficiently low-lying to retain moisture. Much of this terrain is capable of intensive cultivation on the basis of one crop a year. During periods of drought *tierras de humedad* suffer more than irrigated land, while in especially wet years they are, like irrigated land, subject to flooding. *Tierras de humedad* make up something under 2000 hectares.

Temporal (about 7260 hectares) is mostly hill slopes. In good years a reasonable crop may be produced from *temporal* land, but the hazards of farming it (and the work involved) are much greater than those presented by either irrigated land or *tierras de humedad*. Erosion can also be something of a problem and it is not unusual for soil to be washed away and for crops to be lost in the case of an especially heavy downpour. Constant use of *temporal* land depletes its fertility, consequently, fallow intervals must follow every third or fourth year of cultivation.

Temporal shades off into *monte* (17,667 hectares), which is unsuitable for agriculture. This is high, steep, stony ground with very little topsoil. In part it is woodland used for the collection of firewood and the making of charcoal. A certain amount of rough grazing is available on the *monte* and poor peasants may send a few goats or one or two head of cattle into the *monte* to struggle for a bare existence. A few corn *milpas* (small field or patch) dot the *monte*, but these are one-shot efforts on the part of the very poor to harvest a meager crop. It is always highly uncertain whether a crop sown on the *monte* will ever be harvested.

Those who cultivate the *monte* use the slash-and-burn system. This entails the cutting and burning of the natural cover and on steep slopes almost inevitably leads to erosion. The line of cultivation is every year creeping higher and higher up the mountain sides.

On the valley floor cultivation is now, and has been for generations, based on the plow. Animal drawn plows pulled by mules or horses are still a fairly common sight, but increasingly these are giving way to tractor drawn machinery. As the commercialization of agriculture increases, greater use is being made of tractors and other modern implements. This is especially true on privately owned land, but even *ejidatarios* are finding it possible to rent machinery, or in some cases, even buy it.

INDUSTRY AND COMMERCE

Agriculture remains, as in the past, the mainstay of life in Zamora. Recent developments in Zamora, in particular the establishment of new processing plants, do not radically change the picture since the bulk of new industry is geared to processing agricultural products. There is no evidence that historically Zamora was ever an important industrial center. A certain amount of spinning and weaving—essentially cottage industries—is attested to in nineteenth-century sources. Two or three water-powered flour mills are known to have been in operation prior to the introduction of electricity early in the present century, but these were small operations and did little to alter the agricultural nature of the local economy.

Although the local economy is still based on agriculture, the last 30 years have witnessed the introduction of several small industries. Initially these industries were for the most part directed toward the transformation of local agricultural produce to meet regional market needs. Increasingly, and especially in the course of the last five years, the orientation has been toward national and international markets. Thus, for example, the very important strawberry freezing and processing plants, of which there are now a dozen in the *municipio*, ship around ninety percent of their produce directly to the United States. In 1958 there was not a single freezing plant in the *municipio* and the relatively small strawberry crop of the period had to be trucked out of the *municipio* for processing and marketing.

Even with these new developments, more Zamoranos make their living as farmers and farm workers than in other kinds of employment. In 1958 about half of the economically active population of 13,000 was engaged in agricultural activities while under 2000 workers, about 500 of whom were in modern industries, earned their living in small workshops and factories.

During their peak periods of operation, the strawberry freezers now employ as many as 10,000 seasonal workers, while perhaps 1500 *zamoranos* hold steady factory-related jobs. These are important changes which we shall examine in more detail in the final chapter. But agriculture remains dominant. It employs 8,772 Zamoranos out of the 1970 total of 20,861 economically active citizens of the *municipio*. The temporary workers in the freezing plants are almost all drawn from sectors of the population that would otherwise not be wage earners, mostly women and girls from low-income groups. For employers this has the advantage of relatively cheap labor, while for the individuals and families so employed, the extra wages are the chief incentive.

COMMERCE AND TRANSPORTATION

Mestizo peasants and Indians from neighboring communities come periodically to Zamora to purchase at the stores and the municipal market. Zamora merchants

Street scene outside the municipal market.

Campesinos *sowing a crop of chick peas. Mechanized agriculture is becoming more common, but most small farmers still rely on mule or horse teams.*

trade in food staples and finance seed, fertilizer, and implements for the *campesinos* and *ejidatarios* of the valley and the surrounding regions. By advancing money and other items for next year's crop, merchants are in a strong position to control the production. They influence what the small farmer will grow and typically purchase crop surpluses at harvest time.

The activities of merchants and the role of Zamora as a major market center have been greatly aided by a good system of communications. Even in 1958 the road network linking Zamora to satellite communities and to larger cities was reasonably adequate. The artery of the Mexico City–Guadalajara highway was a good all-weather road. Connecting roads, which a dozen years ago were gravel and dirt, have been substantially upgraded. There are more and better bus connections between Zamora and the hinterland and services to Guadalajara, Morelia, and Mexico City have also been improved.

Indian and *mestizo* peasants come to Zamora from as far as sixty miles away. The standard means of transportation is the second-class bus, a rather ramshackle vehicle prone to frequent breakdowns, but falling within the financial means of all but the most impoverished. On Sunday afternoons, following the major weekly market, lines of Indians and *campesinos* may be seen at the bus stop near the municipal market ready to carry home the produce they have not managed to sell or the goods they have purchased. The combination of people and articles reflects the juxtaposition of the modern and the traditional: an old *campesino* draped in a plastic sheet (the poor man's raincoat) holding on to a brace of reluctant chickens; a young Tarascan mother with her child asleep in the safety of her *rebozo* somehow managing to balance a half-full basket of cherries on her head, while her other hand firmly grasps a transistor radio loudly playing the latest Mexican hits.

The Yurecuaro-Los Reyes branch of the Ferrocarriles Nacionales (National Railroad) unites the *cabecera* with an extensive rail network. Prior to the construction of good roads, the railroad handled a substantial passenger traffic, but most people now prefer to travel by bus. This link is however important commercially. It is via the Zamora railroad station that much of the frozen fruit finds its way to North American markets. As much as twenty American refrigerator cars may leave the Zamora sidings for points north in a single day.

EMPLOYMENT, UNEMPLOYMENT, AND STANDARDS OF LIVING

Although the *municipio* is currently enjoying something of an economic boom, income distribution is very uneven and there is a substantial degree of unemployment and underemployment. Prior to 1964, when the Mexican-United States farm labor agreement (Public Law 78) was terminated, many *campesinos* went to the United States as contract labor for periods ranging from several months to a year or more. This is no longer possible, although men still try to get into the United States illegally, some succeeding and some failing.

In 1958 an official of the *presidencia municipal* estimated that 4000 men of the *municipio* had only temporary work or none at all. There is little reason to believe that this figure has decreased. In 1958 minimum wages protected by federal legislation were 9.60 pesos. Current minimum wages are 25.50 pesos, an apparently substantial increase, but one that must take into consideration the higher cost of living. "The peso," as I have been told, "does not go as far as it used to." The current rate of exchange of 12.50 pesos to the U.S. dollar may not give a true picture of the purchasing power of the peso in Zamora, but even the most optimistic estimates of the cost of living make it evident that 25 pesos and 50 centavos provide for only a bare subsistence. Five mangoes cost a peso; 25 centavos will purchase one slice of pineapple or a quarter of a watermelon; *tortillas*, the staple food of the poor, cost 1 peso and 30 centavos a kilo, and five kilos can easily be consumed by one family in a day. Meat and canned goods are much more expensive. The cheapest pair of factory made pants cost 10 pesos.

At the other end of the economic scale is a relatively small group of *ricos*, the rich, who control most of the commercial and industrial life of the *municipio*. Rich by any standard, even to the degree of owning their own private planes—the latest status symbol in Zamora—they are the plant owners, the large merchants, and some of the *pequeños proprietarios*. The richest of the *ricos* have substantial interests in all three fields: industry, land, and commerce. The citizens of the *municipio* recognize this small group as the controllers of economic affairs. Depending on one's estimate of how much wealth one needs to be considered a "*rico*"—the estimates range from forty to sixty individuals and their respective families—a huge gulf separates the poor masses from the few rich.

Between the very rich and the poor is a middle group made up of small shopkeepers, government employees, teachers, and some professionals. In most cases these are not landowners, but pretty strictly urban people, people with steady jobs and occupations, but essentially of a subordinate nature. In the past it had proved possible for enterprising individuals of peasant background to enter this middle group, especially via small-scale trade. This was especially true of the period following the Revolution, say between 1915 and 1935. It would seem that today, and for sometime past, class mobility has become harder and class lines more rigidly drawn. As one informant phrased it, "Today, whatever you want to do, it is a question of formal qualifications, of education and permits." The fact that the speaker is himself rich and of humble *campesino* background (being rich and established are sufficient qualifications) gives credence to the statement.

3 / A brief history of Zamora

FOUNDATION

According to local tradition, Zamora was founded in 1540 as a military outpost of the kingdom of New Spain. The original charter of the town has long been lost and the exact date of founding is therefore in doubt, but the traditional date may be somewhat too early for there is good indirect evidence in the form of land grants, which usually accompanied the establishment of new settlements, that the town was founded around 1574. Documents in the Mexican National Archives indicate that in that year forty Spanish soldier-colonists were given lands in the vicinity of Zamora. The grants in question were not especially large, certainly not the great estates which some *conquistadores* acquired as rewards for the conquest of the Indies, but rather what the Archives refer to as *caballerias*, estates a little over 100 acres. It seems likely that most of the colonists were natives of the province of Leon in Spain, as the name of the settlement was taken from a town in that province, and the river on whose banks the settlement was built was named the Duero, a stream which also flows through Spanish Zamora.

Zamora was organized in much the same way as other Spanish frontier settlements of the period. The colonial administration regarded Zamora as a military post (at that time all adult male colonists had the obligation to bear arms) controlling a potentially hostile Indian region. It was also expected to guard against raids from the northwest, an area not yet under Spanish control.

The Spanish colonists in Zamora followed the standard colonial practice of "reducing" the scattered Indian settlements into one or more large concentrations of Indian population. The Teco Indians (a branch of the Uto-Aztecan Teco-Tecaxquin) living in the valley are mentioned several times in early documents. Around 1750 this Indian community, then numbering only thirty families, was officially joined to Zamora as a *barrio* of the town. In all likelihood, the Teco Indians were by then already feeling the pressures of cultural assimilation, and sometime in the early part of the nineteenth century they ceased to exist as a separate cultural component. Today, their old *barrio* on the edge of town is still called *barrio del Teco* and it retains a vestige of its former separate identity in the plaza which once was the center of *barrio* life.

At the time of its foundation, Zamora must have been a settlement of 120 to 160 Spanish inhabitants holding sway over a much larger number of Indian

21

peasants. We can assume, given the nature of the colonial situation, that from its inception the community was divided into two classes, a pattern that in broad outline continued for the next 350 years. At first there must have been little difference in the size of the landholdings granted to different colonists. Although much more wealthy and much more powerful than the surrounding Indians, it appears that the founders of Zamora were relatively modest folk of provincial origin, probably themselves peasants who had come to the New World to better their fortunes.

However, even within a few years of the settlement of the town, a trend toward some concentration of property was underway, for by 1577, a dozen of the original founders had sold their property and left for other areas. Information on the developments of Zamora during the seventeenth century is very scanty. We assume that a small but steady increase in population took place. There is no evidence that the town was ever called upon to repel an Indian attack or was ever in any danger. By 1746 the population had increased to some 300 families, which, if we allow five individuals per family, would give us a total of some 1500 individuals. In the year 1782, 414 tribute payers are listed on the town rolls, but since both married and unmarried men paid tribute, the total population is harder to assess.

NINETEENTH CENTURY

With the nineteenth century we are on firmer historical ground. The earlier part of the century was still a period of relatively unconcentrated landholding; there were some large landowners, but also many smallholders. However, by the end of the century most of the prime land in the valley was in the hands of a small group of property owners who are still locally referred to as the "aristocracy." Small-scale subsistence farming was virtually limited to poorer hill lands, while most peasants had little option but to hire out as laborers on the estates of the rich. Between rich *hacendado* and poor *peon* there was a relatively small group of merchants and artisans.

Evidence is clear that at least some of the *hacendados* had interests other than those in and around Zamora and owned properties in other regions and real estate in such cities as Guadalajara and the national capital. *Campesino* informants stress that many of the old landowners lived neither in Zamora nor on their *haciendas*, except perhaps for a few months in the year. The picture one gets from most peasants is that of a rich and powerful group, somewhat distant from local life and local problems, and primarily interested in maximizing profits in order to live a comfortable life in some distant city. Even allowing for some exaggeration, the old aristocracy was evidently a well-to-do and fairly sophisticated *rentier* class. It was not unusual for *hacendado* fathers to train their sons in the manner peculiar to their age and class: they were sent on the European "grand tour" to acquire the correct gentlemanly polish and many attended institutions of higher learning, mostly in Mexico, but in at least some instances in Spain, France, or Italy. One member of this elite was educated in a well-known English public school which, of course, are private and expensive.

The day-to-day management of properties was typically left to agents who resided permanently in Zamora or on the *hacienda*. This individual might be hired on a fixed salary or, more frequently, depend for his livelihood on a percentage of the profits realized in the course of the year. The *capataz* or *mayordomo*, as this man was termed, has come down in local folklore as a particularly cruel and avaricious character. Peasants who at one time lived under *hacienda* conditions generally manifest far stronger hostility when discussing the role of these stewards than when talking of the actual landowners. These, of course, were the men the peasant came most into contact with in the course of his life, men who for the most part were recruited from the *campesino* class. Furthermore, while the Revolution dispersed the *hacendados* and ultimately confiscated much of their land, the superintendents sometimes achieved new power positions.

In reconstructing the life-style, behavior, and attitudes of this prerevolutionary landowning class, we find it difficult to avoid the oversimplification with which this period now tends to be viewed by most present-day Zamoranos. Since it is now more than fifty years since the *hacienda* system was fully operative, time has blurred the memory of those men who as young *peones* formed part of the *hacienda* organization. For most of the inhabitants of the *municipio*, the heyday of the *hacendados*, which coincides closely with the rule of General Porfirio Díaz (1876–1911), is something which comes out of history books or of which they are reminded by political figures on anniversaries of the Revolution.

There still lives a minority of people—considerably smaller now than was the case in 1958—who remember the years before the Revolution as an age of law and order and of strong, but just authority. "In those days," I have been told, "you could leave a purse of gold coins in the plaza and nobody would touch them." Certainly, criminals were given short shift and those bandits and robbers who were apprehended by the Rurales (a police which guarded the rural areas) and other authorities were chained together and sent to the Islas Marias and other penal colonies. As an object lesson to other potential evildoers, the prisoners were paraded under military escort and marched from the town plaza to the railroad station. Other informants stress that this was a time free from political corruption and without the current economic uncertainties. A small landowner of peasant background, assured of the confidentiality of his opinion, insisted that the old days were not nearly as bad as some would make them out to be.

> Not many remember the days of Don Porfirio, but do not believe everything you are told. A man willing to work had a chance to get on and whatever he earned was safe. Money was worth something then, it was not this filthy paper [taking a bunch of dirty and dog-eared peso notes from his pocket and waving them with disgust], but *real* money, gold and silver.

This opinion, however, is not shared by many. For every modest Zamorano who feels that things have gone downhill in the past half century, there are dozens of others who regard the past as a period of unmitigated exploitation. The *hacendados* are described as monopolizing all those things that make life worthwhile, not simply wealth, but also health and education. Much more common are reactions like those of an old *ejidatario*:

> At the time of Don Porfirio we were worked like beasts, from sunup to sundown. If we did not work hard enough to please the *capataz* we were beaten, or even run out of the hacienda and could get work nowhere else, for no other hacienda would employ a dismissed peon. We often went hungry, pay was not enough to meet bodily needs, and the plots which they gave us for growing our own food were too small. Anyhow, we seldom had time to work them. When the *patron* came to the hacienda all the *peones* and their families had to receive him joyfully—who would dare to complain of cruel treatment with the *mayordomo* standing by?

The problem of reconstructing this past is hampered by the fact that the old *hacendado* class has practically disappeared from the region. It is also unfortunate that perhaps the only bona fide former *hacendado* in Zamora was not inclined to cooperate with my researches.

THE ROLE OF THE CHURCH

Zamora has a long history as a Catholic stronghold in what is considered one of the most religious states in Mexico. Since the foundation of the town, the church has been very influential in local life, not only in the strictly religious sense, but also in education. The fact that in 1862 this relatively small country town was chosen as the seat of a new diocese indicates its importance in the eyes of the church. It is somewhat difficult to evaluate the role of religion in the everyday life of Zamoranos half a century ago. The more conservative elements of the population assured me that prerevolutionary Zamora was characterized by strong religious adherence on the part of all segments of the population. Local tradition is certainly replete with miracles and apparitions: in 1850 a cholera epidemic was brought to a halt through collective prayers and special services; in 1886 special papal dispensation was obtained to crown an image of the Virgin in nearby Jacona; a divine apparition of the Virgin is recorded for 1914, and shortly afterwards, when a Revolutionary general attempted to dislodge a statue of Christ from its place in the cathedral, he was struck senseless before he could carry out the act. Religiosity is attested to by the numerous and impressive churches and the unfinished new cathedral which was begun early in the century but never completed because of the Revolution. As one Zamorano phrased it with not a little pride, "When we go to the United States we are impressed by the excellent public buildings, the great hotels, and the fine restaurants. Our churches, however, are superior."

But this is only one side of the coin. In interviews with peasants and *ejidatarios* I was told that in the old days the priests were hated by the *peones* and the poor, for they acted hand in glove with the large landowners and the rich. According to these informants, priests sanctioned the punishment of recalcitrant workers, preached obedience to the status quo, and were not averse to tipping off the authorities regarding forbidden activities among their parishioners. One man stated that in those days the clergy acted "as spies for the *hacendados* and were thus seldom trusted by the *peones*," while another informant hinted that the sanctity of the confessional was not always observed—what you said to a priest did not necessarily stop there. There is little doubt that the church, here as in other parts of Mexico, had vested interests in the established order and that on the whole it stressed the traditional in social, political, and economic matters. Of course, one should point out that distrust of the clergy, and envy of the political and economic power of the church, must not be equated with anti-Catholicism. The same men who fulminate against what they consider to be the abuses of the clergy see nothing illogical in defining themselves as Catholics. Virtually everyone in Zamora identifies himself as a *creyente*, a believer. The rituals and usages of Catholicism—the saint's days (every one celebrates his *santo*, the day of the saint he is named after), the baptisms, the first communions, the weddings, and the eventual final rites of death—are so thoroughly interwoven into the fabric of the culture that it is difficult to say where the religious ends and the profane begins.

THE EVOLUTION OF INTERMEDIATE GROUPS

Long before the Mexican Revolution there lived in Zamora individuals who were neither members of the aristocratic landowning class, nor landless *campesinos*, employed on the *haciendas*. With the model of a three-part class system (upper, middle, and lower) readily at hand from the history and sociology of complex Western societies, one is tempted to call this a "middle class," but it was primarily an in-between component made up of two distinct entities lacking shared goals or a basis for common action. The origins of this non*peon*, non*hacendado* segment must be sought in the nature of the colonial society in which positions of power were monopolized by a small elite group.

Originally, culturally Spanish and biologically European, the directing elite in time lost its genetic distinction, while concurrently, close and continued contact between Indians and Spaniards led to the cultural disintegration of the aboriginal communities (the Teco Indians) and their transformation into *mestizo* Spanish-speaking peasants. While this process was not accomplished overnight, it must nevertheless have been well underway by the end of the sixteenth century. These genetic and cultural changes, however, did little to alter the relationship between the dominant group and the peasant mass; whether Indian-speaking or Spanish-speaking, the peasantry retained its position of subordination.

The fact that in due course biological distinctions between the rulers and the ruled virtually disappeared is a circumstance of no great social importance, for in New Spain society was primarily structured by social and cultural, rather than biological, variables. The cultural assimilation of the Indians was, of course, important in one respect. It meant that the peasantry of Zamora, however socially inferior to the *hacendados*, was not regarded as Indian. Indians lived a life apart, while Spanish-speaking peasants to some degree shared in the European-derived culture which was then taking root in Zamora and other localities of substantial Spanish settlement.

It is in this context that we must seek the role of intermediate groups, their origins, and their development. While a social structure based on the *hacendado-peon* distinction (essentially a two-class colonial system) evolved as a consequence of the Spanish conquest and became entrenched in colonial and prerevolutionary Mexico, the needs and requirements of the directing classes could not be fully met by a subordinate peasantry, but also required the presence of specialists who were not of the *peon* class. In a town like Zamora, this category would include merchants and shopkeepers, minor officials and lesser clergy, with a sprinkling of individuals in the professions and the semiprofessions. This sector, which in due course evolved into a more clearly defined middle class, had an established place in town life. It not only met some of the local needs of the *hacendados*, but also provided a number of the goods and services required by the peasant population.

However, a sanctioned group of this nature could not by itself meet all the demands made upon it. The very fact that it operated as an appendage of a system which was administratively centralized, economically rigid, and, even at the best of times, bureaucratically cumbersome, limited its scope of operation. Under such conditions, it is not at all unusual for parallel organizations to come into being, organizations that are more flexible and that typically are little concerned with formal legality.

This, in fact, is what occurred in colonial Mexico, which was a standing temptation to smugglers and illicit traders of all kinds. The very rigidity of the colonial system allowed for the development of all kinds of marginal elements lacking a socially sanctioned place in society—itinerant merchants, horse traders, contrabandists, and mule drivers. In all likelihood, these colonial operators represent the ancestral model for the *arrieros* (muleteers) which worked the Michoacán back country half a century ago, and can still be found in some numbers in the western part of the state. Many stories are told in Zamora about the activities and adventures of the *arrieros*. Often contrabandists themselves, they had informal understandings with the leaders of *bandolero* (bandit) gangs, who in many cases, especially during periods of strife, were the real rulers of the regions through which they traveled.

Guile and accommodation were the keys to such encounters. Payment to bandits was thought of as a business risk and counted as a normal business expense: so many pieces of *manta* cloth, so much gunpowder, so many pesos. For the mule train operators it was a kind of protection, while for the *bandoleros*, a steady income was assured if one was not too greedy. "The good businessman," I have been told, "made a deal." Only as a last resort did an *arriero* shoot a bandit.

In cultural background the *arrieros* had much more in common with the peasants than with the Zamora middle class. However, their economic orientation was regional rather than local. The Zamora middle class may be regarded as an essentially urban group in a rural setting, still retaining many rural values, but certainly not peasants. On the other hand, *arrieros* and other marginal types were rural in outlook and orientation. They should, nevertheless, be distinguished from the *peones* by the fact that they were not *hacienda* hired hands and probably would have fitted badly into a *hacienda* setting.

In conclusion, on the eve of the Mexican Revolution, two groups or entities can be distinguished in Zamora besides *hacendados* and *peones.* One is what we have called the Zamora middle class, locally oriented and traditional; the other is a marginal group of peasant background but characterized by considerable independence.

ZAMORA AND THE REVOLUTION

On the 15th of September, 1910, Mexico celebrated the centenary of its independence. The government of Don Porfirio seemed stronger than ever. The peso was solid, the Rurales kept order in the countryside, political dissidents were either in prison or exile, and law and order was the motto of the day. In Zamora, the event was celebrated with due fanfare. There were fireworks and parades, bicycle races, and 300 poor children were given a free meal. A new fountain was dedicated.

But in Zamora, as elsewhere, it was the end of an era. Six months later Porfirio Díaz had resigned the presidency and the country was about to enter a generation of chaos and warfare. The years of unrest, from 1910 to the early 1930s, brought insecurity and hardship to most *zamoranos*. Conservative individuals, in particular some of the long-established storekeepers and merchants, tell how this was a time of arbitrary and unpredictable rule (although the town was never the scene of a major battle, it did change hands numerous times), poor communications, and such chaotic currency that even the *municipio* had to issue its own notes.

It was during this period that the land redistribution program was put into effect. In the *municipio, ejidos* were officially established between 1924 and 1939, but long before these years considerable disruption of the traditional order had already occurred. The Revolutionary armies which crisscrossed the countryside were, in the main, peasant armies, and the common soldier fought chiefly for land. The promise of land and freedom from the oppression of the rich and powerful— the *tierra y libertad!* (land and liberty) of Zapata's soldiers—offered a more tangible reward than political franchise, electoral reform, or even national unity.

The breaking up of the *haciendas* and the redistribution of these estates to the peasants became the key to peace in the countryside and a reestablishment of national stability. In Zamora, however, many *campesinos* did not apply for land. In the words of one *ejidatario*,

> They were men who had for many years worked in fear of their masters and therefore did not dare to ask for land under this new program. They were afraid that if they took land in this manner, the old landowners on coming to power again—for many feared that this might come about—would severely punish them for their action.

It has been suggested to me that the clergy were to some degree responsible for this fear. There may be some truth in this since the church was anything but cooperative with what it viewed as atheistic and socialistic programs (other things besides land reform were involved). The *Cristeros* (a Catholic counter-revolutionary movement) were very active in the Zamora region, and these activities led to government measures of reprisal.

Whatever the causes, it thus came about that a number of those who applied for land and got it were not true *campesinos* at all but individuals with no training in agriculture. Nevertheless, many *campesinos* did get land, although at times in rather unusual ways. On realizing that the estates were about to be broken up, some landowners decided to make the best of the situation. If possible (although this was against the law) they divided their holdings among members of the family in an effort to keep as much land as possible under their control. Should this prove difficult, they might call upon some of their most trusted peasants (the overseers, for instance) and present them with a portion of land—if the land was going to be taken away, it might as well be given to those one most liked. Thus men who had never owned land were suddenly masters of their properties.

There were many opportunities during this period of uncertainty, when land prices fell, *haciendas* were abandoned, and the agrarian reform program was in its infancy, for shrewd or well-placed men to gain control over substantial holdings. Men who were granted land but did not wish to work it, could rent it out to those who wished to farm it, and all kinds of "deals" were possible. A small farmer neatly summed up the process when he said, "In those days, a man who went to bed as a *peon* might, through shrewdness or good fortune, wake up a *don*."

Still, with all its imperfections, and there were many, the agrarian reform program did bring about a major shift in landholding patterns. This entailed not only a change in ownership, but also a change in land-use. Where previously the large estates were geared to a national market, initially the 4-hectare plots which were granted to the *campesinos* became subsistence holdings devoted almost entirely to the production of foodstuffs for home consumption. This, as we shall see, was to change following World War II and a reorientation to cash crops, but it took some years for this change to come about.

Aside from land, the times were such that opportunities were not lacking for the adventurous or the astute to take advantage of the economic uncertainties then prevalent. Zamora is full of stories detailing how the most prominent men of today—or increasingly in 1971, the founders of prominent families—started off on the road to fortune. Most of the tales hint that the line dividing the legal from the illegal was often trespassed. It is not always possible to check these accounts, and even though there may be an element of envy in their telling ("regardless of how important he may be today, so-and-so after all started off as a smuggler"), the stories are less malicious than laudatory. The man who can outwit others, especially officials and outsiders, has nothing to be ashamed of in rural Mexico, and most of the men in question are of *campesino* background.

The majority of these men, who fit pretty closely the archetypical *arriero* pattern which we have previously examined, were not born in Zamora but in small pueblos somewhat removed from the city. In origin, they are certainly not part of the Zamora middle class. No doubt, the very traditional and conservative mores of the established middle class were not conductive to innovation and risk-taking. In contrast, many poor hill villages of Michoacán can boast a long history of *arriero* trade. In short, the Revolution not only distributed land to the peasantry, but made possible the emergence of new and economically powerful individuals. The *hacendados* vanished from the scene, the middle class remained a middle class, while the vacuum caused by the disappearance of the *hacendados* was filled by new men, men for the most part with little formal education, but with much drive and a solid knowledge of local conditions.

4 / The cultural frame

IDENTITY AND CULTURAL UNITY

While the *municipio* of Zamora does not lack internal social divisions—there is never any question that the *ricos* and the *acomodados* (well-to-do) live in a style very different from that of the *pobres* (poor)—major cultural cleavages are absent. However, it would be wrong to imagine that all *zamoranos* are culturally alike. Cross-cultural differences of the kind that separate Indians from *mestizos* are absent, but *zamoranos* recognize that wealth and education, and that attribute which they refer to as *cultura*, which for the moment we can translate as "refinement" or "background," are not evenly distributed throughout the population. All *zamoranos* share some cultural attributes, but the inhabitants of the *municipio* also evidence subcultural differences according to class and education. In short, Zamora is to some degree a microcosm of national society with its peasants and townsmen, its rich and poor, its unschooled and educated.

One may ask a *zamorano* the simple question "What are you?" In most cases this will bring a ready response, although spontaneous identification in terms of class is rare. This is not because class differences are not recognized, but because the common vocabulary does not readily lend itself to concepts of this kind. The typical *zamorano* will identify himself and others in terms of residence, economic standing, individual social position (rather than class membership), or occupation. Thus, a man is unlikely to be referred to as a "member of the upper class," but rather as a *"rico"* or as a *"distinguished zamorano."* At the other end of the social scale, we find such terms as "the people of the *barrios bajos*" (the poor, or "low," neighborhoods), a *"campesino humilde"* (poor peasant), and a *"vendador ambulante"* (a peddlar).

"CULTURA" AND THE REMEMBRANCE OF THINGS PAST

The most common term of identification among the commercial and industrial elements of the population—that is, those who are not poor *campesinos* or working-class urban people—is simply *"zamorano,"* inhabitant or native of Zamora. The significance of this term is understandable only if we take into consideration its special connotation for those who use it.

29

It is clear from the way *zamoranos* speak that Zamora is thought of as much more than a simple geographic location, one's home town, either by birth or adoption. Zamora is, as the local phrase has it, *"la sultana del Duero,"* a title that may be given the literal but essentially meaningless English translation of "sultaness of the Duero." In order to grasp something of its emotional dimension, one should conjure up an entity incorporating the features of beauty, majesty, magnificence, and warmth. Orators sing her praises on the occasion of *fiestas patrias* (national holidays), while local poets, of which there are a number, write verses lauding her beauty and fertility.

Elementary school girls at school fiesta. They are dressed as Indians, an attempt on the part of the school authorities to develop a sense of national integration.

It is seldom, though, that such feelings lead to concrete acts of community improvement, such as efforts at improving crumbling sidewalks and the inadequate drainage system. In fact, Zamora and especially the older sections of town, are badly in need of renovation, but the *zamorano* will not concern himself with traits having to do with poverty, dirt, or inconvenience: The *sultana* has no blemishes.

"Sweet Zamora, we exalt and glorify thee," writes a local poet, and in his eyes, and those of other "cultured" *zamoranos*, the city is endowed with the usual superlatives. The climate, one is told, is healthier than that of other regions, while life in Zamora is especially pleasant. But such feelings of local pride are of a kind that one might expect to find in any small town. Typically, the allusions contain a much more personal component. The feelings evoked are those of *amor*—love— for the Villa de Zamora, a love that is filial. In the words of one *zamorano*, "in her tenderness she has sheltered those who have come to her in times of need and difficulty."

What does Zamora represent for those who view her in this quasi-material role? First, it represents Christianity and all that it implies in a highly traditional *mestizo* region; secondly, those features of Hispanic culture that distinguish the city dweller from the poor *campesino*, and originally, the Spaniard from the Indian.

Once more, terms of address and reference give a clue to the underlying emotions. Zamora is spoken of in phrases echoing religious devotion—"Zamora de San Martín" (patron saint)—and a colonial past—"Zamora de Nueva España"; "Zamora de la cruz y de la espada" (of the cross and the sword); even, "Zamora de los conquistadores."

The *zamorano* thus sees himself as heir to a long tradition derived from Spain and the Catholic church. The superiority of this cultural tradition is never questioned. True, the Indian is not always thought of in an entirely negative manner and there are those *zamoranos* who profess respect for Indian customs, but there can be little doubt that the Indian is typically thought of as inferior. The Indian is amusing. He speaks a strange tongue—hardly to be thought of as a language—and when he uses Spanish he is likely to make comical mistakes in pronunciation. It is generally assumed that he is inherently dull, perhaps even of subnormal intelligence, and on very little evidence, his habits are branded as "dirty" and he is by *mestizo* definition *sin cultura*, without culture.

Although under normal circumstances the Indian is not thought of as especially dangerous, he is believed capable of working himself into a state of great anger and frenzy, especially when under the influence of alcohol. One is therefore "never sure" how an Indian will react ("they look so quiet sitting in front of the cathedral, but . . ."), so the wisest policy is to have as little to do with him as possible. Patronizingly, he is often spoken of in the diminutive, *indito*. Perhaps the whole attitude is summed up in a conversation I had one market-day morning with some young *zamoranos*. They had seen me taking photographs of vendors and customers in the market, some of which were Indians and others *mestizos*. The last few shots were of an Indian woman and her daughter selling cherries. One young man asked me whether I was especially interested in Indians, to which I answered that I was taking pictures of everyone. "But," the young man exclaimed, "these are only *inditos*, they are not *zamoranos*. What will your friends in the United States think when you show them photographs of such ugly people? It would be wrong for them to think that we look like that."

The *zamorano* will readily refer to himself as a *cristiano*, a Christian. This entails much more than membership in a Christian church or sect. It not only signifies some active or passive involvement with the Catholic religion, but also identifies the individual in a total cultural sense. A *cristiano* (one is very much tempted to say a "real" cristiano) speaks Spanish and leads the local variant of Spanish-derived culture. Religious affiliation is not of itself the only important criterion. An Indian may be a baptized and participating member of the church, but according to common usage he does not rank as a *cristiano*, regardless of the strength of his religious feelings.

A *zamorano* is thus, ideally at least, a person with *cultura*, an individual who has at least some education, or, lacking specific educational credentials (preferably a university degree), at least an appreciation for the past and a willingness to nurture tradition in the present.

In what is still a predominantly rural and small-town setting, one meets the opinion that the life of the big cities is not quite wholesome. Said one *zamorano* recently returned from a visit to the capital, "A trip to Mexico [City] is very exciting [he mentioned movies and night clubs], but it is no place to bring up a family." A suspicion of metropolitan life is not unusual in inhabitants of small towns, whether these be in Mexico or elsewhere. The big city does have attractions and the *zamorano* does recognize that Mexico City or Guadalajara are more "modern," but in his opinion this modernity is acquired at a price that he is not willing to pay.

Somewhat harder to understand is a selective process that screens out those aspects of the Michoacán scene that do not conform to middle- and upper-class small town cultural patterns. This became clear to us during our efforts to furnish our Zamora apartment. In part because it was cheaper, and in part because we enjoyed it, my wife and I made use of furniture and household implements of Tarascan and *mestizo* village derivation: woven mats (*petates*) for the floor, hand-made beds and chairs, beaten copper pots and pitchers, earthenware bowls, and various textiles for drapes and coverings. Our *zamorano* friends were so thoroughly fascinated at this novel example of interior decoration, that they came many times (and brought their friends) to visit and examine. Comments ranged from "very original" to the not unkind "your house looks like a museum." Obviously, they had seen nothing like it. It soon became evident to us that for many *zamoranos* an item crafted forty miles from the town is almost as foreign as if it had been made in Mongolia or Tierra del Fuego (in contrast, items manufactured in the United States are in great demand).

"WE, THE POOR"

The attitudes so far examined are restricted to a relatively small sector of the *municipio* population. To identify with the supposed glories of Zamora and the mystique of a Hispano-Christian colonial heritage requires some combination of education, wealth, and interest in things past not found among the poor and the common people, the *pueblo*. Again, we have to keep in mind the restricted meaning of *zamorano*. There are many poor people in the *municipio* and the *cabecera* (small artisans, factory workers, laborers, *ejidatarios*, and so forth) who are geographically and politically *zamoranos*, but who culturally lack the attributes we have described. These people do not allude to the town as a keeper of tradition, nor do they evidence much interest in the distant past. They care nothing for *conquistadores* or the civilizing mission of the church.

What they do share is a common poverty, a condition that binds them to the poor of the nation rather than to the elite and middle classes of Zamora. That they live and work in Zamora or one of the surrounding communities is relatively inci-dental; Zamora means essentially that their families and friends live on a particular street or in a particular *barrio*, that they work for some *patron* of the town or, if

A poor working-class or campesino *mother and child. Mother is wearing a* rebozo *around her shoulders.*

fortunate, cultivate a strip of *ejido* land somewhere in the *municipio*. Though they speak Spanish as their mother tongue and generally follow the rituals of Catholicism, these are facts that warrant little comment. Asked about such things, a poor man is likely to reply that "for us it is natural," and perhaps throw in a comparative observation to the effect that "in the United States they speak English and there are many Protestants." In no sense does speaking Spanish and being a Catholic bring to mind visions of Spanish colonists conquering the region and establishing the civilization of old Spain on the banks of the Duero River.

The *pobres* of Zamora then—a term signifying not solely poverty of resources, but a paucity of *cultura*—have much more in common with the *campesinos* of the little *mestizo ranchos* (hamlets) than with the bourgeosie of the town. Within the *municipio* the basic style of life of the poor varies little according to location—in their words, "we eat the same *frijoles* (beans)." A life that in many cases is close to bare subsistence permits of few refinements and little distinguishes one poor man from another. Food, clothing, and habitation decrease in variety as one goes down the economic scale. At the very bottom, stripped of everything but the bare necessities of life, these people know a material and spiritual oneness: "we, the poor"; "those who labor."

Constant preoccupation with survival leaves room for little else. Problems tend to be met as they arise and goals are short-range. The distant past is dismissed as having little bearing on present-day needs; the future is reduced to the horizon of a few weeks, months, or perhaps the length of an agricultural season. It would seem that the very shallowness of this temporal perspective blunts the localism of the poor. A poor *campesino* is likely to refer to himself in terms free of narrow associations, perhaps simply as "a poor man," maybe as "hard-working *campesino*."

If at times there is a metropolitanism of the rich, as seems to have been the case with the prerevolutionary *hacendados*, economic circumstances may also conspire to make the less fortunate aware of much that they hold in common with their fellows. Few are the families that have not contributed one or more male members of the *bracero* groups which periodically leave for seasonal employment in the United States.[1] There *campesinos* of the *municipio* meet workers from all parts of the Republic and surely realize that they belong to an entity larger than the local *rancho* or the town *barrio*. In the *municipio* a tradition of work in the United States has grown over the years. Economically, this is an important feature of *campesino* life since it helps to absorb surplus labor and helps maintain *campesino* families.

However, work in the United States has another, if related, function. It is a means by which men acquire a substantial amount of prestige among their fellows. Tales of work in the United States—"on the other side," as it is often referred to— seem never to lose their interest. Middle-aged men will tell youngsters how really tough it was to work on railroad maintenance gangs in the state of Washington during the hard winter of 1944; how cold the snow was, how punishing the labor. But the pay was exceptionally good "because they needed Mexicans to keep their railroads running since all the Americans were away fighting the Japanese." Younger men then describe present conditions, including the risks of crossing the border illegally. Good contracts and bad contracts, good bosses and those who exploit Mexicans, all are remembered in *campesino* anecdotes. But whether lucky or unlucky, the man who has labored in the United States gains a definite status by the mere fact of running the risks and facing the consequences.

NATIONALISM AND NATIONAL IDENTITY

Unlike many of the communities studied by anthropologists, Zamora is neither a tribal enclave nor a village of isolated peasants, although the mass of *municipio*

[1] Prior to 1964 when the *bracero* program was terminated.

inhabitants are peasants and others are of *campesino* origin. As a component of a complex national society, it is inevitable that *zamoranos* give some thought to their identity as Mexicans and also to the place of Mexico in the community of nations. It is not that questions of nationalism are uppermost in the thoughts of *zamoranos*, but still political and national issues are not strange concepts. Given the opportunity, *zamoranos* will readily verbalize about Mexico, its form of government, its national institutions, and even draw comparisons between Mexico and other countries, in particular the United States.

However, being Mexican means different things to different segments of the population. Thus, the established middle class tends to stress those features of national life most in keeping with its traditional orientation, for instance, Catholicism and a deep veneration for the Virgin of Guadalupe as a symbol of all that is best in national tradition. As a group, it distrusts foreign ideas and foreign innovations, especially those that are considered to be "corrupting," but this distrust is not extended to the material products of our age, whether these be automobiles or such other tangibles as refrigerators and household appliances.

The new economic elite shares most of these attitudes, although perhaps less keenly. Here anxieties are more on economic grounds: fear of competition and the potential loss of regional market privileges. In somewhat the same way as the established middle class fears the encroachment of cosmopolitanism, be it national or foreign, the new rich, *los ricos*, define the enemy as "big business," which includes both large Mexican corporations and American affiliates.

Overt nationalistic manifestations in the form of set-piece celebrations are a common feature of Zamora life. As such *fiestas patrias* have all the characteristics of being anything but spontaneous, it is difficult to assess their value as an index of underlying emotions. As is generally the case in other Mexican small towns, the most vocal participants at such celebrations are government officials, schoolteachers, and some of the professional people. These are the individuals who deliver the speeches and organize the parades. The bulk of the population play a relatively passive role. Speakers launch into long, complex discourses of economic and political theory, history, and international relations, and it apparently makes little difference that much of what is said is aimed at a level well beyond the comprehension of the average listener ("statistics tell more truth than words," "today [1957] Mexico is behind eighteen other countries in economic development, but we will be fully industrialized by 1960").

It is difficult for the outside observer to ignore the bored peasants brought by truck to the central plaza or not notice the lines of children fidgeting away a morning as one long speech follows another. The fireworks which usually terminate such occasions and the musical interludes which punctuate the speeches are enjoyed by all, but this would probably be true of any fiesta. It would be wrong, however, to imagine that nationalism is nothing more than a fabrication of *politicos* and orators. The *campesino* mass—the very individuals who seem most apathetic during regimented shows of "public solidarity"—evidence in private conversation an acceptance of their part in a nation-wide entity. Their *mexicanidad* is definitely different from that of politicians and intellectuals; it lacks perspective or theoretical formulation, but at the same time is mostly free of the defensive-aggressive undercurrents which are a feature of the nationalism of other sectors. We may say that it is a nationalism that is worn easily, without doubts or over-burdening anxieties.

It is unlikely that anyone, regardless of class or occupation, remembers the kind of speeches that typify *fiestas patrias*. There are occasions, however, that apparently remain engraved on the memory of *zamoranos* long after the events have passed into history. *Campesinos* have described to me in considerable detail the tactics used by Pancho Villa in 1917 at the time that he was running circles around General Pershing's Punitive Expedition following Villa's raid on Columbus, New Mexico. My informants had not participated in these events, but they had heard of them from other peasants. The point of these stories is that Villa was a very wily *guerrillero* who was able to outfox Pershing's force, although, according to them, Pershing tried everything from airplanes to Indian scouts in his attempts to corner Pancho Villa. Middle-class *zamoranos* tell other stories, less heroic perhaps, but no less indicative of how they feel as Mexicans. Thus, in 1914, when American Marines landed in Veracruz, young *zamoranos* flocked to the *palacio municipal* and demanded arms to repel the invader. At the same time Zamora merchants showed their anger by throwing into the street American-made goods, one druggist breaking so many bottles of American patent medicines that the episode is still vividly remembered by some older citizens.

The villain in many of these stories is the United States, whether it be in 1914 or in 1938 during the oil nationalization crisis. However, attitudes toward the United States are by no means totally negative. It is true that Mexican nationalism has to a large extent been forged on the fires of American foreign policy, but if these past episodes are remembered, it is no less true that the United States offers a model of the good life that many would like to aspire to. A *campesino* who has worked in the United States for wages that few Americans would even consider working for, will in all sincerity say that there is much that is good in the country, that

> there a man who is not afraid of working can do something with his life. His children will always have enough to eat, his wife can have a gas stove to cook on and a refrigerator to keep the food. People are respected for what they do and it is not a question of whom they know.

Whether this is a valid observation is not the point, but I have little doubt that most *campesinos* of the *municipio* would agree with the statement.

More sophisticated *zamoranos* are unlikely to echo such wholehearted support for the United States, but even a young university-trained professional will concede that

> it is inevitable that our technology must come from the United States. There is much that we must borrow from you, but what is important for us Mexicans is that we retain our integrity and our right of choice and selection.

ZAMORA AND THE NATIONAL POWER STRUCTURE

Behind a facade of representative government, the Mexico of Porfirio Díaz was governed by and for a small segment of the population. Locally, this meant that national policies favored the *hacendados* and that local government was either in the hands of this elite or of those directly working for it. Postrevolutionary Mexico is different in a number of respects. Out of the turmoil of the Revolution there emerged one political party, the *Partido Revolucionario Institucional*, or PRI, which for more than thirty years has maintained a monopoly of power. Mexico is far from being a classic democracy, but the organizational structure of PRI does allow some flexibility. Ideally, the party is "collegiate," which is to say that different "blocs," or interest groups—peasants, professionals, bureaucrats, workers, businessmen, and so forth—have a role in establishing policies. I say ideally, because any political party that has been in power for well over a generation tends to lose touch with the people, or as one *zamorano* observed "we now have a situation where sons follow their fathers in politics in much the same way as a son used to follow his father's trade or profession." In short, party and government are one and indivisible. Government is highly centralized and run by a large bureaucracy that links the smallest village to the national capital, while elective office is virtually restricted to PRI candidates.

Zamora, being second in population only to the state capital of Morelia, is a unit of some political importance. It has become the home of numerous government agencies and departments: highway police, *Pemex* (the national oil corporation), the department of hydraulic resources, government banks, courts, military garrisons, and other entities. Consequently, there reside in Zamora numerous individuals working for state and national organizations and dependent upon these systems not only for their livelihood, but also to some extent for their social position. The power structure of civil servants and politicians is thus of more than local importance. Policies and orders come down from Morelia or from Mexico City, and even the municipal government is far from being an autonomous agent (the key position of *secretario municipal*, municipal secretary, is an appointed office). Throughout the pattern is one of hierarchical control, with every head of department or minor official being responsible to his *jefe* or boss, the ultimate boss being the president of Mexico.

The whole political-administrative setup is a power structure, the ultimate sources of power being outside the *municipio*, but the local representatives enjoying amounts of power and prestige commensurate with their positions within the system. This graduated hierarchy easily establishes the most important individuals: the heads of departments and agencies. Subordinate to these are the individuals who fill intermediate posts in the bureaucracy, and these officials are in turn backstopped by a bevy of minor functionaries and underlings.

What should be understood is that all spheres of public life have a bureaucratic facet; poor and rich alike, the inhabitants of Zamora deal frequently with government and its agents. The range is extremely broad. A *campesino* seeking a contract to work in the United States must first get clearance from the municipal authorities; businessmen must obtain the necessary permits to manufacture, sell, and ship their goods; farmers must, or at least should, comply with regulations governing soil and water conservation; births, deaths, and marriages must be certified or solemnized before the proper authorities.

We do not imply that all *zamoranos* follow the letter of the law; in fact, there is a good deal of covert law-breaking that is widely known but causes little comment. For instance, it is illegal for a private individual to lease *ejido* land from a *campe-*

sino, and for a *campesino* to rent out his land. Yet everyone knows that this is taking place all the time, that a number of *ejidatarios* prefer to rent their fields rather than work them.

However, the penetration of government into everyday life is readily observable. To cite but one example, primary school graduation exercises are attended not only by pupils, teachers, and parents, but also by the authorities. In a specific instance, these included the *presidente municipal*, the commandant of the Zamora military garrison, and the district representative of PRI.

While the bureaucracy impinges on the life of everyone, contacts and relationships vary enormously depending on the individuals involved. The upper levels of the bureaucracy have little to do with the mass of the people; it is the minor officials who reserve their ministrations for the *campesinos* and the poor. On the other hand, no Zamora entrepreneur or merchant need concern himself with office subordinates—he moves ahead to see the man in charge. Consequently, bureaucrats tend in their official, and by extension, personal, dealings to align themselves with the class with which they come most into contact: upper level officials with upper-class individuals, minor officials with poor and lower-class people. In Zamora, as elsewhere in Mexico, one goes as high as rank permits by using contacts, position, or whatever other lever one can bring to bear. That a rich and important citizen can get an immediate appointment to see the *presidente municipal*, while a poor man has to wait in line to have his case or petition processed by a clerk, is regarded as entirely natural, or at least causes no comment.

5 / The structure of Zamora society

UNITY OF UPPER-CLASS AND MIDDLE-CLASS VALUES

The social structure of Zamora is not especially complex. The outsider soon learns to distinguish three broad class categories: the *ricos*, the established middle class, and a lower or working class. Pressed to align individuals on the basis of *"clases sociales,"* social classes, *zamoranos* will come up with roughly the same distinctions, although, as previously noted, they will typically use different terms, generally those associated with wealth or occupation.

Zamora social classes are primarily defined by wealth, although other factors such as education and family background are secondary criteria. The fact that the upper class of Zamora—*los ricos*—have adapted their style of life to that of the older established middle class virtually eliminates attitudes and cultural values as a means of differentiating the upper from the middle ranges of society. In many societies middle classes attempt to model their style of life on that of the upper-class elites, but in Zamora the situation is reversed. The old elites vanished with the Revolution, leaving behind the middle class as the only viable model for emulation by new rising groups. Consequently, the *ricos*, the majority of whom are of *campesino* origins, assiduously copied the "cultured" behavior of a highly conservative small-town middle class.

An individual who belongs to neither the new rich nor to the older middle class—say an urban factory worker or a *campesino*—no doubt perceives both groups as powerful and wealthy in contrast to his own poverty and insignificance, but although culturally very similar, the two groups are economically distinct.

The *ricos* are not only individually wealthy, but they also control the economic life of the region. While this control may not be absolute, it is sufficiently powerful to have given rise to the widespread belief that only economic endeavors with the tacit support of the rich have a chance of prospering in the *municipio*. The elite also enjoy a virtual monopoly of the elective political offices of the *municipio*, in particular the key post of *presidente municipal*.

"LOS RICOS": THE LOCAL UPPER CLASS

The rich generally have so much more wealth than others in the *municipio* that even a newcomer to the town has few problems in recognizing who they are. Also,

39

most of the *ricos* are fairly recent newcomers to the town, individuals who have come into prominence in the course of the last generation. The group itself is very small, at most 200 individuals, counting not only the "important men," but also their immediate families. The smallness of the group probably accounts for the ease with which it rapidly assimilated the cultural patterns of the middle class.

Although Zamora "society" prizes the values associated with *cultura* and an identification with the putative grand past of the town, manifestations of these values come remarkably cheaply. As minimum requirements, we can isolate a style of life that is definitely not peasant and interest, generally shown by some financial support, in perpetuating the image of Zamora. For most *ricos, cultura* does not require a personal involvement in intellectual pursuits. The cultural ideal may be that of the educated man capable of conversing on a variety of subjects; a man who knows something of the outside world but also has a deep appreciation of the local past. But the fact is that few *ricos* have the necessary training and erudition to fit the model of the cultured gentleman. For these individuals, a few thousand pesos invested in the patronage of some local writer will more than compensate for shortcomings in education and experience. An alternative is to undertake some charitable task, for instance, support a church renovation program or provide money for the maintenance of an *asilo*, a home for the aged or orphaned.

In terms of tangible symbols, the *ricos* of Zamora give considerable importance to a large and well-furnished house, "well-furnished" should be understood as a quantitative rather than qualitative term. The houses of the *ricos*, and of the middle class, are furnished in a mixture of styles with "modern" tubular steel furniture, pseudo-French provincial, and heavily upholstered Victorian pieces co-existing in the same room. Status is gained by having a library or study with several shelves of books, although these are to be admired rather than read. Titles run heavily to Spanish classics, history, and biography. Surrounded by his library ("I'm too busy to do much serious reading") the *zamorano* of this class is likely to confine his leisure time reading to *Selecciones* (*Reader's Digest*), *Life en Español*, and the newspapers.

Perhaps surprisingly, since clothes are often a mark of social position, the most prominent *rico* males dress quite casually. My impression is that since all *ricos* are personally known within the town and the surrounding region, it is not necessary for *rico* males to dress with any special care. It is also probable, given the *campesino* origins of many upper-class *zamoranos*, that they simply do not feel very comfortable in suits and ties.

THE MIDDLE CLASS

In contrast to the *ricos*—few in number, easily identified, and all men of local importance—the middle class of Zamora comprises a wide range of economic and occupational categories: small landowners, professionals, shopkeepers, employees, and, shading off to the lower class, self-employed artisans and store clerks. Some enjoy substantial prestige irrespective of their economic position (most of those engaged in part-time literary pursuits would fit this category), others are men of minor consequence in the community, the *petite bourgeoisie* of small storekeepers, clerks, and office help.

A rough division is recognized as separating the professional or professionalized group from artisans and small shopkeepers. In part, this division is based on economics, but an even more important factor is education and *cultura*. The lower middle class—if we may term it such—is less polished and generally manifests a high proportion of lower-class and peasant traits in such areas as food habits, housing, and attitudes. In their speech—an important category—they are hardly distinguishable from lower-class people. However, we should note that the lower middle class is mostly self-employed and generally enjoy independent assets in land, premises, or equipment. They often employ one or two assistants and usually engage in activities requiring a certain degree of skill.

The upper levels of the middle class embrace individuals with relatively fixed

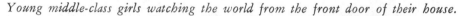

Young middle-class girls watching the world from the front door of their house.

incomes and an educational background of at least secondary school and occasionally university. Income varies, but tends to be sufficient to maintain a "decent" style of life. No one works with his hands and most people aspire to a set of ideals emphasizing a steady conservatism compounded of home, job, family, and *cultura*.

THE LOWER CLASS

In Zamora no one has trouble identifying what are variously called the poor, the working people, the *peones*, or simply the "humble" members of society. There are of course degrees of poverty—from the abject poverty, or *miseria*, of those who must survive on a day-to-day basis and have a few marketable skills, to the relatively secure livelihoods of *ejidatarios*, skilled workers, and small subsistence farmers.

It seems likely that in time an established working class will emerge in Zamora; a class with steady jobs, some education, reasonable security, and perhaps even a degree of group consciousness. But for the moment, most members of the lower class continue to live in an unpredictable and capricious world. One day work is available, another it is not; today there is enough to eat, but no one can be sure that the same will hold true for tomorrow.

Still, the lower class is not all cut from the same economic cloth. Of those who work on the land, the *ejidatarios* are a category meriting special attention. A few, those who are either most fortunate, hardworking, or successful in their business dealings, live well enough. For the majority, life is a hard struggle, but not a struggle without hope.

The relative security of the *ejidatario* (a function of *ejido* titles) contrasts with the extreme insecurity of the landless *campesino*, who is often at the mercy of his employers, the *pequeños proprietarios*. Even today, *pequeños proprietarios* are in a position to exert all kinds of pressure, such as demanding that "their" farmworkers remain faithful to them by not accepting alternative employment. Should a *peon* be tempted to work for someone else, he may find himself blacklisted by the original employer and never again be hired by him. This threat is real enough in the context of the local employment situation: there are simply not enough agricultural jobs to go around, and given the pressures of rising population, this state of affairs is unlikely to change until opportunities in industry are vastly improved.

In somewhat the same favored position as the *ejidatarios* are the skilled and semi-skilled town workers, those who in the local parlance have a definite *oficio* or trade. Some are employed in factories, others in small workshops. This group may in due course form the nucleus of the established working class we spoke of earlier, but the group is small and lacks organization.

Much less fortunate are the unskilled workers, men such as the *cargadores* who unload produce trucks and can be found wherever some menial or physically demanding job is in the offing. They can be hired by the load, the hour, or if fortunate, the day. It is impossible to live any length of time in Zamora without coming into contact with such individuals. When jobs are scarce, poor men go from house to house soliciting work of any kind—"*Patron*, do you have any work for me today? Do you want your car washed, does the lady of the house need help in cleaning the windows?"

For the unskilled and unfortunate of the lower class, unemployment or under-employment are predictable hazards. To some extent, even the distinction we have drawn between those with a little land and those without is partly a matter of semantics. Given an *ejidatario* family which includes a father and two or three adult sons—by no means an unusual combination—should the two sons be regarded as landless, or as part of a family work team engaged in exploiting the family's four hectares of land? Obviously, there comes a point where the family *ejido* can no longer support all the members of the family no matter how reduced the subsistence level. Even so, family ties being what they are in rural Mexico, it is most un-likely that anyone in the family will be denied a share of what is extracted from the land. Attempts may be made to find employment elsewhere, often work of a temporary nature, but this is done without prejudice to the rights of the indi-vidual to part of the family income. The family *ejido*, or private smallholding (some of which are no larger than *ejidos*), remains "home" for any member of the family.

Even the unemployed are seldom without some means of support. Once again, family loyalties and family networks provide a buffer against total indigence. If one member of the family is fortunate enough to work, his income will be utilized for the benefit of family and kin, not only offspring and wife, but often brothers and sisters, parents too old to work, or grandchildren, as the situation demands. It is perhaps in part for this reason that the person most pitied in Zamora is the individual *sin familia*, without a family. A large family is a sort of folk insurance scheme, especially important to members of the lower class, but operative also, in terms of contacts and connections, among the elite and middle sectors of society.

This pattern of "family cooperatives" is a hedge against misfortune, but it does not solve all problems. I have sat with *campesino* families trying to decide on whether they can afford to send their children to school. Often, it is not a simple question of whether the children will go to school or not, but which children will go to school and for how long. School is theoretically free, but there are many fringe expenses, for books, for bus fares, for the proper clothes, which, for poor families, add up to a very heavy financial burden.

The problems of sending a child to school are symptomatic of the whole vicious circle that keep the poor poor and the members of the lower class at the bottom of class structure. It costs perhaps 1000 pesos a year to send a child to school, and yet it is only through education, and the credentials that education provide, that many poor children can hope for a better future.

THE INTERPLAY OF POWER AND WEALTH STRUCTURES

The two structures in the *municipio*—the system of class alignments based primarily on wealth and the intrusive hierarchy based on politics and government—must necessarily function together in a common setting. The two structures are often so closely interwoven that any attempt to establish strictly independent

Three campesino *generations. The young man on the right has recently returned from the United States (note dress and the two watches he is wearing).*

A door-to-door seller of song birds in a middle-class neighborhood.

parallels distorts reality. For instance, the *ejidatarios* are part of a system of federal control and direction. Not only is the land which they work and over which they exercise use-rights government land, but, at least ideally, they are organized into *comunidades agrarias* which are corporate entities falling within the orbit of PRI control. Also, *ejidatarios*, again more in the realm of legal fiction than reality, are accountable for the way they work their land to the ministry of agriculture and its agents. Yet the *ejidatarios* are all local peasants who work their land in much the same way as other smallholders and depend on *cabecera* merchants and other Zamora capitalists for cash loans and other arrangements to see them through the agricultural year. Of course, the *ejidatarios* are a rather special case, but what is true of *ejidatarios* is true in some degree of all who work for the government. Even those who regard themselves, or are regarded, as birds of passage, holding down a job in Zamora for the length of a government assignment, must find their level in the system of class alignments.

Most professional or professionalized civil servants associate socially with individuals of similar training and backgrounds; technicians, doctors, lawyers, and other middle-class *zamoranos*. This may be done with a certain degree of condescension, the feeling that Zamora is "very provincial" and that middle-class *zamoranos* are "conservative and old-fashioned." However, while the commitment to local mores is far less total than for those whose lives center around the community, non-*zamoranos*, whether government employees or ordinary citizens, have little difficulty in fitting themselves into the local system. For all its peculiarities and anachronisms, Zamora, does, after all, form part of the national culture, and its class structure can in large part be duplicated in other Mexican towns of similar size. In much the same way as administrators and other functionaries find their niche in the local middle class, lower-level government employees—janitors, policemen, and such—are incorporated into the lower class. For the most part these are native *zamoranos* who simply "work for the government."

The merging of political and class hierarchies is most complete at the upper levels of local government, especially in the case of the key office of *presidente municipal*. The law stipulates that the *presidente* and councilmen (the *Ayuntamiento*) must be elected by popular ballot every year. The realities of political and economic power restrict the *presidencia* to wealthy men with good PRI connections. Consequently, the highest elective office of the *municipio* has become the virtual monopoly of some half-dozen individuals who move in and out of office with a regularity that approaches clockwork.

The fact that a few *ricos* control the *presidencia* does not pass without comment, but even those who envy the wealth and power of *presidentes* concede that affluence may render them less prone to temptation. This attitude is well brought out in the statement of a *campesino*, who, after complaining that everything in Zamora was controlled by a handful of rich men, answered a question concerning the honesty of politicians in the following manner: "Most officials can be bribed, but it is different with regard to the *presidente municipal*. Of course he works for the interest of the *ricos*, but who can bribe a millionaire?" In Mexico, as elsewhere, a great temptation to graft is poverty, and while poverty (or at least expectations higher than one's salary) is almost universal among the ranks of the salaried civil servants, *presidentes* in Zamora are not hampered by this disability.

This does not mean that *presidentes* are especially progressive or especially popular with the masses. They tend to be viewed as men with the vested interests of class, an evaluation that contains a good deal of truth. In a way, this is somewhat paradoxical. PRI, the official government party, claims a commitment to social justice and the general welfare of the people, but in Zamora its highest representatives tend to be men of great private wealth whose social philosophy is diametrically opposed to official government policy.

STATUS DETERMINANTS

If power, economic and political, is the major determinant of class position in Zamora, a number of secondary factors affect the standing of individuals in the community. These refer more to status than to class, to the way that individuals are judged as individuals in terms of an already established frame of reference. For instance, a child born of upper-class parents is by definition a member of the upper class, but being a child, his status is very low, so low that one might almost say he has no status. On the other hand, a poor landless *campesino*—just as surely a member of the lower class as the child in question is a member of the upper class—may, because of his agricultural knowledge, industry, and advanced years, be regarded with honor and respect by all those who know him.

Sex and age are recognized status variables. The sexual division of society is such that males are accepted as the natural heads of families (*jefes de familia*) under whose direction the household group operates. Furthermore, all important leadership functions are in the hands of males. Women (in a manner not unlike children) are not outside the class system, but, being subordinate, take their place in society from their parental families, and when married, from their husbands. It is true that a middle-class woman married to a peasant is described as having come from a "good family," perhaps a "family of good name." She does bring to her marriage something of her original class membership. Nevertheless, the very fact that she did marry a peasant is in itself highly indicative. In the majority of cases it shows that her family was either marginally middle class or that it was in the process of losing, or had already lost, much of its middle-class position. In another society it might be unwarranted to make predictions of this type, but as we shall see in the next chapter, middle- and upper-class *zamoranos* seldom enter into marriage without express family permission. Thus to marry "below" (for either sex) is an indication of downward mobility—the family could not find a better match.

Age alone is seldom sufficiently important to guarantee status. It is true that respect is shown to the old, but in the majority of cases it is not so much an accumulation of years that makes an individual worthy, but rather certain concomitants arising from a long life span. *Zamoranos* of all walks of life emphasize that years bring forth experience. Certainly, in many of the more traditional occupations engaged in by the citizens of the *municipio* no noticeable advantage is enjoyed by youth over those of more mature years. To have lived many years means that one has made many contacts and learned much of local conditions; the old man is to some extent the man who knows everybody. This explains in part why many family businesses employ a kind of apprenticeship system. The father will teach his son not only the techniques of storekeeping, accounting, production, and so forth, but will also make sure that he gets to know the suppliers, clients, customers, and such other individuals as are important to the business. Agriculture, especially small-scale agriculture, operates in a similar manner. The son learns by following the father at the plow, by hearing him talk of crops and seasons, of *monte* and *tierras de humedad.*

That traditional occupations such as agriculture and shopkeeping should employ such a learning process is not too surprising since it is just such methods of learning, and more broadly of cultural transmission, that account for much that is traditional and customary in preindustrial societies. Less expectable is the fact that the new industrialists of Zamora think and act in much the same way. It should be remembered, though, that they are on the whole self-made men, individuals who have learned from experience rather than in schools and universities. As such, they feel that no education can rival that which life itself provides. Furthermore, their field of operation is typically a regional one which means that personal contacts and personal knowledge count for much. It is not that these men are against technical training and education, which in the abstract they praise highly, but that they are not products of such a system. Their point of view is well summarized in the statement made by one of their number, "Given time a man can learn anything."

Cultura, which we have already had occasion to mention, is a very important status marker. *Cultura* is not so much formal education as measured in years of school attendance or in formal qualifications such as degrees and diplomas, as the kind of knowledge that the "cultured" man possesses. Certainly a man that has attended university is regarded as a man with *cultura,* it being assumed that he has learned much, that he is *culto.* But what must be understood is that any individual can manifest *cultura,* regardless of his formal training. *Cultura* is expressed in speech; it is apparent in manners; it may even be shown in the way one dresses or the furnishings of one's house.

To a considerable degree *cultura* is a cultural code peculiar to the *mestizo* way of life. Indians, coming as they do from a different cultural tradition, do not have it, and they are therefore described as *incultos, sin cultura.* The concept has deep roots in the colonial past and derives ultimately from the dichotomy that differentiated Indians from *mestizos,* who in contrast to Indians referred to themselves as *gente de rason,* the "rational" or "thinking" people.

Although in contrast to the *inditos* all *mestizos* are to some extent *cultos,* individual *mestizos* manifest different degrees of *cultura.* Virtuosity in the Spanish language is perhaps the minimum requirement and one to which all *mestizos* can to some extent aspire. Every occasion which is somehow worthy of note is celebrated with speeches and recitals. These may be purely private functions, such as weddings or saint's day celebrations, or more public occasions, such as national holidays and religious ceremonies.

If the spoken word is highly valued, the written word is even more so. There are a number of part-time writers in Zamora. These include a historian, a biographer, a geneologist, and a poet, all of whom have published. Two other men, a novelist and a poet, hope shortly to enter the literary ranks. None of these men engage in writing for financial reward, and none may be considered of more than local importance. The material for their books and verses is all local; their intellectual interests reflect a traditional viewpoint; and much of what they write could as easily have been penned in the nineteenth as in the twentieth century.

In a world of mass communications, it comes as something of a surprise to find that geneologies of local families, histories of regional miraculous Virgins, and biographies of municipal worthies continue to be considered fit subjects for literary efforts. But Zamora writers write for a limited and local readership and acquire local prestige in the process. Erudition of this type is highly regarded: A man who has written a book is referred to as an "author"; an individual who has contributed articles to a local magazine or newspaper is by the same token a "journalist." It matters little that one works in a bank and the other in a government office, the preferred title is the literary one. In many instances, these works are subsidized by local businessmen who in this manner show their patronage of the arts and gain a reputation as *cultos*.

Status may be enhanced in still other ways than those already examined. Charity and philanthropy bring respect, as do simple competence and hard work, sobriety, and leading a decent life. A mother who sacrifices and works hard to look after her family is spoken of as a "good woman"; a competent farmer, even if not a rich man, gains status by his knowledge. To this list, which could be lengthened indefinitely, one might add the compassionate priest and the doctor who treats the poor without a fee.

All these qualities which we have referred to as "status" do not go under a single name in Zamora. The *zamorano* speaks of "respect," of an individual being *culto*, considerate or well-mannered. These are personal qualities which, in theory at least, are to some extent independent of wealth or class position. It is certainly possible to be both rich and lacking those attributes which add up to a favorable opinion on the part of one's fellow citizens. One man of considerable wealth in fact fits this category: He is described as "without sentiment," totally uncouth ("like a mule") and lacking both public spirit and personal redeeming qualities.

The honorific that most clearly designates status is *don*, and except by flatterers, it is used with some care. A *rico* will most likely be addressed as such, as will a professional man or an individual who is obviously *culto*. But there are rich young men and young professional men who are referred to simply as *señor*, a perfectly polite but more neutral term. While a man of mature years is more likely to be *don* than a young fellow, age alone does not confer the title. It is generally age in combination with dignity, sagacity, or competence that merits the appellation.

GROUPS AND ASSOCIATIONS

Unlike North American communities which abound in service clubs, patriotic organizations, PTAs, Scouts, and similar groups and associations, Zamora can almost be considered a society without formal groups and clubs. This lack of associational activity, whether it be for the purpose of entertainment or for more serious goals, is no doubt related to the dominant position of the family and the importance of person-to-person, or dyadic, relations in Zamora.

Entertainment and relaxation, indeed the whole field of recreation (apart from spectator sports, going to the movies, and so forth), is virtually a family preserve. Those families who can afford it celebrate life-crisis situations, weddings, saints' days, first communions, and the traditionally important fifteenth birthday of a daughter, with elaborate parties to which family and close friends are invited. These functions have a ritual quality and tend to generate an atmosphere marked by restraint and formality. Among the upper and middle classes, there is no such thing as a party for a party's sake—a lesson we learned in attempting to reciprocate a number of invitations and then finding it necessary to invent a "reason" for the occasion.

Such gatherings bring together both sexes and all ages, but polarize along sexual and generational lines, married women gravitating to a specific corner, adult men congregating to discuss local problems of business and politics, adolescent girls monopolizing some part of the patio. Only young children seem free of restraint, while in contrast adolescents and even young unmarried adults behave more as spectators than as participants. At no time do young unmarried men and women mingle freely together.

Spontaneity and originality are the exception. Conversation is formalized and polite, and all forms of uninhabited boisterousness are clearly regarded as bad form. Entertainment, if provided, is of a similarly restrained and formal nature: The daughter of the house may grace the occasion with a piano recital (traditional Mexican airs, some light classical pieces), or a friend of the family known for his virtuosity may render some well-known sentimental piece of poetry such as *La Muerte del Bohemio*, a long poem detailing the death of an artist in his garret.

Very similar *fiestas* are described in the "literature of manners" from nineteenth-century provincial Spain and in more contemporary ethnographic reports of small town life in Spain and Latin America. In Zamora, though, celebrations of this kind are not limited to the established middle class but permeate the whole upper and middle strata of society. The evidence indicates that the prerevolutionary upper class, the *hacendados*, which have disappeared as a class, and virtually so as individuals, since the Revolution, were somewhat more sophisticated than the present-day elite. If our reconstruction is correct, we have here a further example of the traditional middle class acting as cultural models for the rising new rich of the community, the rather archaic cast of contemporary high society being explained as a case of "style lag," or to use the term coined by Ernestine Friedl (1968) for a similar phenomenon in Greece, "lagging emulation."

Zamora, it is true, it not without some formal clubs and associations. It has both a Rotary group and a Lions club, but these are not service clubs in the usual sense. Both meet infrequently, and their membership is almost totally drawn from the medical and pharmaceutical professions. Of the six active Rotarians, four are doctors and one an engineer; of the three Lions, one is a doctor and another a pharmacist. These clubs have more in common with a medical association (the impression in Zamora is that they establish fees) than with a businessmen's group. None of the successful entrepreneurs of the town are participating members of either of these clubs.

The one social club is the Club Social. Membership, although not noticeably restricted, is limited to those who can afford an initiation fee of one thousand pesos, which is little enough for a rich businessman but high for those living on fixed salaries. The club numbers around fifty members to whose families club privileges are also extended. The club is neither highly exclusive nor does it bring great prestige. For most of the year the club premises on the second floor of a centrally located building are used mainly by young men to play billiards, dominoes or cards, and drink beer and soft drinks.

Once a year, the club comes into its own. A small orchestra is hired from Morelia or Guadalajara and a formal dance (entry by purchase of a fifty peso ticket) is given. The highlight of the affair is the crowning of the Beauty Queen of Zamora. This young lady, attired in a formal evening gown, is first escorted to her throne by a young garrison officer in full parade uniform. Having seated herself in her appointed place amidst the polite clapping of those present, she is crowned by the club president to the accompaniment of two trumpet fanfares. Next, a special poem written for the occasion by a *profesor* from the secondary school is delivered by its author. More clapping. The president and the young lady then take the floor and after a few solo turns are joined by some of the more intrepid couples. This is the signal for general participation. Throughout the evening, the tone of the celebration remains prim, and while drinks are served, alcohol does not appear to add much zest to the festivities.

The gala occasion we have described is obviously one more manifestation of *cultura*. Just as there are "cultured" behavior patterns for everyday life and for family celebrations, there is also at least one time in the year when the Zamora middle and upper classes come together to enjoy themselves in an appropriate manner. The crowning of the local beauty queen, the formal dance, the speeches and poems, seem to be a provincial echo of what *zamoranos* perceive as "high society" behavior. In fact, when we were invited to this *fiesta*, much was made of the fact that a society reporter from one of the Mexico City dailies was going to be present and would write up the event in his column.

Apart from the Club Social there are a few organizations that cater to special interests. One of these is the Club de Caza y Pesca (Hunting and Fishing Club). As its title indicates, it brings together *aficionados* interested in hunting and sharpening their marksmanship, although apparently it numbers no active anglers. A formal title gives an impression of a formal organization, which is not the case. There are few if any organizational meetings and club members are not required to pay dues. The chief function of the club is to purchase ammunition in bulk at discount prices.

We may note that even this very loosely structured gun club is organized by a civil servant not native to Zamora. This man's fondest wish is to organize a "serious club"; one with a roster of dues-paying members willing to make sufficient contributions in time and money to rent or purchase a strip of land for club use on which a proper firing range could be built and skeet shooting equipment installed. But as he says, "In Zamora many are fond of shooting, but few are ready to take the sport seriously."

There are few organizations catering to the needs of men, but fewer still devoted to the interests of women. There are a number of religious groups in the form of parish associations dedicated to beautifying and decorating church interiors. Most of their activity entails the making of altar cloths and dresses for religious images. A number of younger married upper- and middle-class women engage in charitable pursuits associated with the church. The organization of *kermés* (bazaars) to raise funds for church charities provides an opportunity for convivial visiting and participation in good works. Some thirty young matrons, under the direction of an old and respectable married woman, run an organization devoted to providing school meals for needy children. The members contribute ten pesos each a month and with these funds sufficient milk and bread are purchased to feed the most destitute children in the *municipio* schools.

There is one type of informal grouping that is common among young unmarried men of the upper and middle classes, the group of close friends known as a *peña*. Although according to the standards of North American society young unmarried males lead a very circumscribed life, the amount of freedom which they are permitted is far greater than that enjoyed by young women of the same age and class. This greater freedom, coupled with the restrictions imposed on the opposite sex, probably does much to account for the presence of these groups.

The *peña* is primarily a leisure group composed of about a dozen individuals between the ages of eighteen and twenty-five. These young men spend considerable time visiting each other's—that is, their parents'—houses, going on short outings, getting together for sodas and beers at one of the plaza cafes, and attending movies together. No single interest seems to bind the group, but *peñas* seem to spend much time pondering what to the *jovenes* (young men) are a couple of major problems: how soon to get married and how quickly they can achieve a certain level of economic independence. These two questions are closely related, for marriage in the classes in question demands some very specific economic commitments in terms of income, a suitable residence, and furnishings. Unless these standards are met (or so I was assured) no well-to-do family is prepared to give their daughter in marriage, and, of course, the control of the family over young unmarried women is virtually absolute.

The extremely sheltered life of upper- and middle-class young women prevents them joining together in informal groups of the *peña* type. Girls naturally have friends of their own sex, but seldom meet in groups of more than two or three. While young men have the opportunities to associate in situations outside the immediate control of their elders, no equivalent opportunities are open to young women.

The associational activities of lower-class *zamoranos* are even more limited than those outlined for more affluent citizens. Weddings, births, and so on, do not go without notice, but the scale of festivities is much more reduced. Not surprisingly, there is no lower-class equivalent to the Club Social, and the *peña* appears to be strictly an upper- and middle-class phenomenon. Recreation seems to imply some temporary escape from the pressing problems of day-to-day life. There are movies and soccer games within the financial reach of all but the poorest *zamorano*, and the local *cantina* is in itself something of a club for those able to afford the price of a beer.

6 / Interpersonal and intersexual relations

THE IDEOLOGY OF MALE SUPERIORITY

While groups and associations other than the family play a relatively small part in Zamora life, interpersonal relations outside the confines of formal groups take on a major significance for *zamoranos*. The people of the *municipio* are highly conscious of themselves as individuals and the local culture has much to say on how they should behave as such. Behavior is based on a code of values and expectations which defines ideal roles for both men and women. One of the keys to understanding this code is the division of the sexes, a division which not only offers guidelines for intersexual relations, but has some degree of applicability in all interpersonal contexts.

From infancy, the boys and girls of Zamora are trained to lead radically distinct lives. Parents and other authority figures lose no opportunity to reinforce and reward behavior and attitudes deemed suitable to the sex in question, and discourage manifestations considered inappropriate. In this early and continued emphasis on sex-defined roles, the community follows the national pattern, and more broadly, similar patterns common to Mediterranean and Latin American societies.

Child training practices, the formal educational framework, adult roles, and employment opportunities all act to reinforce the myth of male supremacy and female subordination. The selective process starts early. Thus, a little upper-class boy of some two years of age who hits his mother in a fit of pique, or makes a nuisance of himself by upsetting the routine of female kitchen help, is not rebuked or punished. Rather, his mother, with a show of pride at the antics of the little imp, will turn to those present and smilingly say, "Isn't he growing quickly into a little man?" Guests are expected to agree and add suitable comments about how husky he is becoming. In much the same manner, a little girl who shows the feminine virtues of decorum, shyness, and obedience will be rewarded by the approval of her elders.

This early training of children to sex-defined roles and behavior patterns is more apparent among the middle- and upper-class segments of the *municipio*, but even *campesino* families react in similar ways. I well remember two *campesino* children, not over six years of age, one a boy and the other a girl, playing in the mud a short distance from the boy's house. The children were making mud pies,

52

or, as they are called in Zamora, mud *tortillas*. As we were talking, the boy's mother looked at her son in some embarrassment. Her disapproval was not directed at the boy's messy state—both children were covered from head to foot in sticky mud—but rather at the nature of the play. "At his age," she told me, "he should be playing with little boys, but he still prefers to play girlish games."

The position of the male is defined as one of dominance and the chief attribute of the ideal male is seen as residing in his quality of maleness, his *machismo* or *hombría*. Certain behavioral and attitudinal characteristics are regarded as the hallmark of the true *macho*. The relationship between masculine character and sexual attribute is direct and overt. Thus, the term *macho* is the common appellation for "male," as well as for all sexually active male animals such as the studs of ranch and farmyard. We may say that masculinity and virility are inseparable; the man lacking aggressive sexuality ceases to be a male, a *macho*, and becomes a *manso*, the docile and gentle castrated animal, the unmasculine man.

THE MALE IDEAL IN FOLKLORE

Machismo is something of a national myth. A considerable body of folklore—songs, stories, jokes, and more recently, the cinema—is devoted to romanticizing this myth. It is perhaps on the screen and in popular ballads that this myth is projected most sharply. In the popular ballads, the *corridos*, the hero is generally depicted as a lover of many women, an individual reckless in his search for new conquests. A recurrent theme is conquest and consequence: The *valiente* (brave one) gives direct proof of his manliness through unrelenting pursuit and subsequent success. But in success there is the seed of tragedy, for success can only be achieved at the expense of some other male, the brother, husband, father, or *novio* (fiancé) of the woman. It is thus not surprising that the *valiente* who consummates his desires seldom lives to a ripe old age. In the *corrido* of Lino Zamora (no relation to the town) (Mendoza 1954: 318), Martín informs his brother Braulio that his best friend Lino is making a cuckold of him:

> When he returned from Jerez
> On Thursday morning,
> His brother Martín said to him:
> "Lino is with Prisciliana."

Braulio takes quick vengeance, and in the next verse:

> On the day fourteenth of August,
> A Thursday, in the evening,
> Lino Zamora was left
> Covered in his own blood.

Another element that often crops up in *corridos de valientes* is the theme of the traitorous woman who, for money or other rewards, will sell a wanted man, perhaps a bandit or a revolutionary, to the authorities or to his personal enemies. The *corrido* of Valentin Mancera (Mendoza 1954: 179) tells how the woman Sanjuana first tricks the hero into lowering his guard,

Sanjuana said to him:
"I shall never forget you,
But put down your gun
And come and have something to eat."

and then conspires with her sister to turn him in to the authorities for the reward he carries:

Virginia said to Sanjuana:
"What do you say, shall we turn him in now?
Three hundred pesos they give us
And with that we make our fortune."

Another *corrido*, that of Benito Canales (Mendoza 1954: 188), ends on a note of warning about perfidious women:

Here ends the *corrido*
Of don Benito Canales,
A woman from Jalisco
Sold him to the *federales*.

The message is clear—even *valientes* have something to fear from women.

The folklore Mexican of the *corridos* and popular stories is modelled on the *ranchero* (cattleman) of the northern half of the republic. He carries with him a number of associations referable to a romanticized historical past, including a cluster of traits that have to do with guns and horses. In reality, this armed and violent man is hardly more typical of the contemporary Mexican than his opposite number, the Western cowboy, is of the American male, but they have in common their presence as images, representations of a certain ideal. As well as being a reckless romantic with a knowledge of guns and horseflesh, the hero of the *corridos*, and of the very popular *ranchero* movies, is above all a man ready to defend his honor, which, of course, requires that he carry a gun. Anything which detracts from his reputation as a man is sufficient reason for a shoot-out, and it is the hero himself who defines when honor is at stake and in what manner it shall be defended.

THE MALE ROLE IN ZAMORA

Turning from a consideration of the idealized male image, and the dangers inherent in the male role, as exemplified in *corridos* and other popular media, to actual examples of *zamorano* behavior, attitudes, and expectations, we notice a number of continuities. Some of these continuities are easy enough to follow since they involve overt traits and attitudes. The male *zamorano*, for instance, typically has a great interest in hand-guns and other weapons. Two gun shops in Zamora do a thriving business and many men own pistols or rifles. Weapons are a constant source of enjoyment, and it does not take long for the visitor to realize that discussing guns is an excellent way to break the ice with a new male acquaintance or revive a lagging conversation with an old one. *Zamoranos*, much like certain North Americans, are quick to point out that the constitution guarantees the right of every Mexican citizen to bear arms.

Ownership of weapons is more common among the upper and middle classes than among workers and *campesinos*. The main reason is probably economic: however desirable, rifles and pistols are expensive toys. Still, there is a sizable armory of firearms, some of truly venerable vintage, in the possession of *campesinos* and *ejidatarios*. Public health nurses, who work mainly with the poorer families of the *municipio*, consider guns a major accident hazard. Part of their routine public health lecture—together with tips on feeding the children a balanced diet and the importance of proper prenatal care—stresses the need to keep father's revolver on a high shelf out of the reach of little fingers.

As for the horse, another item closely associated with the traditional *macho* image, it is true that in contemporary Zamora he has largely been displaced by the motor car. But not so many decades ago, few men of consequences in the *municipio* were without their stable of fine horses. Older men still remember that in 1929 a group of Zamora *charros* (riders dressed in the traditional costume of big felt hats and tight fitting pants and vests) went to Mexico City to form part of the presidential honor guard at the swearing in ceremonies of President Pascual Ortiz Rubio.

Today, however, the automobile seems to have taken on many of the symbolic attributes of the horse. Cars are commonly given names with strong horsey connotations, such as *el poderoso* (the powerful one) and *el bravo* (the spirited one). Trucks and buses often carry messages painted on their bumpers that leave little doubt about the attitude of the drivers. One that came to my notice had all the bravado of a line from a *corrido*: "Me and my brave one, we fear no man." Furthermore, motor cars are almost always under male management, the general consensus being that for a woman to drive is somehow unfeminine. If she does so, she is likely to find herself grouped with the female who smokes or engages in other "male" activities.

Guns and motor cars may, as our interpretations suggest, be symbolic manifestations of masculinity. But masculinity is not without its dangers, and contemporary attitudes, no less than the traditional *corridos*, hint that precautions should be taken. It can be argued that the rigid control of women is in itself a mechanism designed to lower tension and friction—in effect, women are made as inaccessible as possible. This subjugation is rationalized by references to the supposedly uncontrollable sexuality of the Mexican male. In the words of one informant: "We can't allow our daughters to go out alone, they would soon be violated. You must understand that men here are not as they are in the United States—we just can't control ourselves."

Such restrictions—rationalized as protection—keep women from becoming objects of strife, or phrased differently, the male is not faced with the necessity of having to defend the "honor" of his wife or daughters. Even so, women are perceived as potentially dangerous, manipulative, easily tempted, and not very trustworthy. In the background there is always the fear that the system will not quite work as it should, and thus intersexual relations, in much the same way as the broader field of interpersonal relations, carry a high content of anxiety.

With respect to intersexual relations, the theme of the "evil," "grasping," or "dangerous" woman which is reflected in the *corridos* is also apparent in psychological testing. One of the research tools which I used in Zamora was the Thematic Apperception Test, or TAT. This test, developed by the psychologist Henry A. Murray (1943) is widely used as an instrument of psychological investigation to arrive at individual character diagnosis. The subject is shown a series of pictures and asked to elaborate stories as each picture is given to him. The test is "projective" in the sense that the storyteller projects his own feelings into an essentially neutral setting; he should explain not only what is taking place in the picture, but the reactions and feelings of the characters depicted. Psychologists use the TAT to shed light on the personality of subjects—their conflicts, sentiments, and emotions—but TATs can also be used to examine cultural attitudes, values, and roles. A number of anthropologists have used TATs in this manner and the approach is quite similar to that of the analysis of other cultural materials with a "thematic" content such as folk tales, or as we have done in the case of *corridos*, popular songs and ballads.

Our sample is restricted and we make no claim that it is statistically representative. Twenty-eight adult male *zamorano* informants, mostly drawn from the middle and upper classes, agreed to take the TAT (10 pictures, or cards). While another group of *zamoranos* would no doubt have responded in slightly different fashion, I doubt very much that there would have been great disparity in the themes elaborated. The TAT card which is especially useful for shedding light on the relationship of the sexes is Card 4, a card depicting a woman clutching the shoulders of a man whose face and body are averted.

Looking at the roles and emotions ascribed by the narrators to the figures in the card, it is evident that there is far from complete agreement. Some informants see the woman as benign and loving, others as grasping and seductive. With respect to the male, he may be anxious and unsure of what to do next, or in good control of the situation. The most common themes which come out in the stories (a number of different themes may be included in each response, thus a male may be both tempted and determined) are as follows:

TABLE 1   CLASSIFICATION OF THEMATIC RESPONSES

Man	Theme in Percent of Stories	Woman	Theme in Percent of Stories
In conflict	43	Loving, tender	32
Pressure from partner	36	Pleading	25
Angry	25	Dangerous	25
Determined	18		
Tempted	14		
Hostile	11		

Typically, more data is provided on the male figure who is perceived as the chief actor in the drama. The female figure is sketched in more briefly, and generally in relation to how she effects the man's actions. In a great number of the stories the male is faced with some dilemma or conflict arising from pressure put upon him by his female partner. Some choice must be made—to stay or go, to reject or love, to give way to temptation or to fight it—and while in some instances the male is perceived as a determined character, strong and resolute, much more often the problem is left hanging. It is perhaps because of this factor of conflict, and the difficulties inherent in its resolution, that in so many responses the male is depicted as angry.

Most of the narrations are short and quite concrete. It would appear that the *zamorano*, unlike, for instance, the middle-class North American, is not too comfortable in making up imaginary stories. Typically, he describes what he sees and puts emphasis on such factors as the positioning of individuals in the cards, their appearance, the manner they relate to one another (their emotions of the moment), their gestures, and their facial expressions. In many cases, the stories seem little more than stage directions: "This man here, he looks furious. The woman is trying to calm him." Or:

> This is somewhat more difficult, but from what can be seen it is a man who is not letting himself be caught by a woman. She is encircling him and trying to keep him from his wife and children.

In some stories, though, there is considerably greater elaboration, although again, more emphasis is placed on *what* people are doing than on *why* they behave in a given manner:

> This gives me the impression of being an illustration for a short story in some magazines. A love story, and probably the man has to leave the girl for some reason, even though he loves her. She is trying to hold him, but not because she is really in love with him, but rather for her own gain or some reason of convenience. They seem to have been lovers for not too long a time. She has something of an Eurasian look to her, he seems Anglo-Saxon, accordingly the scene probably takes place outside the United States.

Even in stories where the woman is not perceived as dangerous or self-seeking, she is often depicted as attempting to control or influence the freedom of action of the man:

> This seems to be a happy couple. Two young married people. She is telling him to stay; not to go out and do what he is planning to do. He, though, has the intention of leaving and carrying out his plan.

Or:

> A matrimonial scene. She looks somewhat unhappy about something. She is saying to him, "Please don't go away."

Taking the stories as a whole, the dominant theme is perhaps less that the woman is inherently evil, although this crops up with some frequency, and in other cases the goodness or evil of the woman remains unspecified, but rather that she is an able manipulator. Manipulation may be through love, or as in one story, because the woman exerts "an overwhelming attraction" on the man. Fear of manipulation can lead to conflict and anger and these themes, as we have seen, are well represented. The culture insists that men should be strong and determined, dominant over women and in control of the situation, but perhaps deep down most *zamoranos* would agree with the observation of one of my infrmants that "A woman has a hundred ways of getting what she wants; faced with a crying woman a man is helpless and must give way."

HONOR AND "ZAMORANO" PERSONALITY

The *zamorano* sees himself as a man of honor. Honor, as we have seen, is closely linked to a sexual ideal (virility, sexuality, the protection of one's women), but it also has to do with individual reputation in matters and situations that are not overtly sexual. It is in this context that *machismo* impinges on a whole area of behavior that transcends male-female relations. If our analysis is correct, a great deal that has to do with the personality of present-day *zamoranos*, especially those of the middle and upper classes, has its roots in an archaic code of honor and the reactions generated by a fear that this honor may somehow be lost.

The man of honor is the man ready to defend his "name," his reputation, a man with a keen sense of his own masculine virtues, his *hombría*. The key point is that in dealing with others he should not be bested. How he deals with others determines the picture which society as a whole has of him. Preferably, he should deal decently with his fellow men, but above all things he must guard against being made to look incompetent and incapable of resolving situations.

In societies which are structured largely around groups, group membership involves a set of rules and regulations which restrict behavior—something is "done" or "not done"—but also assure protection so long as one operates within the "rules of the game." Obviously, the extent to which cultures define that which is proper, and groups impose restrictions and assure protection to their members, varies enormously. In all cultures, too, there are "gray areas" where the individual is left to his own devices. These are questions of scale and degree. It is not that the culture of Zamora, a subculture of the national culture, is totally anarchic or amoral, but that in contrast to some other societies, the *zamorano* is freer from formal restraints, which also means that he is constantly pitting himself against others. The exception, as we have noted, is the family.

We have therefore a situation in which conflict lurks below the surface, a situation which is inherently anxiety-provoking. Interpersonal relations are marked by overt hospitality and goodwill, a mode which is symbolically expressed in the *abrazo*, the ritualized embrace which signals friendship and is exchanged by all who have more than a passing acquaintance with each other. Together with this though, there is more than a hint of underlying caution and suspicion. Good manners and the use of titles and honorifics seem to indicate a ready disposition to deal with others, but the uninitiated soon becomes disillusioned when offers of assistance and further commitments are coupled with extreme difficulty in getting things done. A special problem is arranging convenient times and places ("Why not come around next week?"). Such devices postpone situations that may not be easily resolved to the satisfaction of all concerned. The atmosphere, though, remains very friendly and the visitor not coached in the cultural ways of the society may go away with the feeling that he has accomplished a fine bit of rapport. No one ever says "No."

The high frequency of such behavior makes it hard to avoid the conclusion that below the level of agreeableness there lurk feelings of reserve, caution, and suspicion. In interpersonal relations this seems to be the functional equivalent to the *zamorano*'s attitude toward women as objects of sexual attraction—overt enthusiasm combined with an underlying fear of too deep an involvement. On the one hand we have a well-developed belief in male superiority, with all its validating mythology of song and story, and yet it is difficult to escape the impression that the claimants protest too much; that behind all the flaunted maleness there is an underlying fear, fear of women, fear for the security of the much advertised masculinity. We find the same puzzling, even contradictory, phenomena in interpersonal relations: manifestations of overt hospitality and goodwill, but along with this more than a suspicion of caution.

CLASS AND FEMININE CONDUCT

In situations of friendship, middle- and upper-class *zamoranos* will talk about themselves and, at least in the abstract, are not averse to talking about women. However, the seclusion in which women live and their fringe position in public life, makes it difficult for the alien male to observe them in the home or among themselves. As is true of many other Latin countries, strangers are seldom invited into the household. Middle- and upper-class *zamoranos* who work in offices, are professionals, or operate their own businesses, typically arrange meetings and interviews (with other *zamoranos* or with visitors from out of town) in their places of business or in public locations such as bars or restaurants.

Besides the difficulty of entrance into the household, observation is hampered by the retiring nature of women, especially in the presence of male strangers. After a very perfunctory formal introduction, it is customary for the wife, children, and daughters of all ages, to retire to another part of the house. They reappear, if at all, only at the moment of departure. Women are present at festive occasions, but as we have seen, family fiestas are very formal gatherings.

The women of poor *campesino* families enjoy noticeably greater freedom of movement and association. In part, this is linked to different styles and different standards of life. For instance, *campesino* families, and the poor in general, usually live in small houses, which sometimes consist of only one room. Also, the women of the poorer classes take a far more direct hand in running their households than do those from more affluent families. The *campesino* housewife, for instance, must personally undertake the family shopping rather than send a servant to the market.

Responsibility comes early to *campesino* girls. In many cases they must look after younger children, help prepare food, and carry out a variety of household duties. This early training in independence probably helps to account for greater autonomy and freedom in later life. It is certainly true that *campesino* girls show more maturity and individual initiative than the daughters of well-to-do families.

Upper- and middle-class women hardly ever engage in any form of independent commercial or business activity. If they work at all, it is always in subordinate posts, such as typists and salesgirls, under the direction of a male. *Campesino* women and lower-class town women are the only real businesswomen in the community. Many of the petty traders of the Zamora market are women who bring in produce from their family fields or who purchase small quantities of staples

Campesino *girls. They are wearing their best clothes for a Sunday visit to Zamora.*

from other growers. Lower-class women are pedlars and small traders in such items as candies and cigarettes.

Upper- and middle-class values having to do with feminine conduct and the position of women are not entirely suitable to lower-class styles of life. The values in question are understood, but simply cannot be applied in the context of the village or the working-class neighborhood. Yet the cloistering of women is a trait—a status marker—observable both among long established middle-class families and the new rich of rural origins. It seems, therefore, that entry into the upper reaches of society is heralded by a general tightening up of control over the women of the family. This change can be read as a statement that a one-time peasant family has moved up in the world.

Motherhood idealized: statue to "The Mother."

Campesino *and his aged mother. In all social classes, motherhood is powerful.*

THE FEMALE IMAGE

In Mexico there is no easily identifiable feminine ideal type which can be likened to the one already described for the male. It is tempting to look to the Virgin of Guadalupe as providing a similar figure for the crystallization of those virtues which the culture regards as eminently womanly. To a certain extent, the patroness of Mexico does have this function, but she appears to be more a man's idealization of womanhood than a woman's blueprint for feminine conduct.

To the Mexican male the Lady of Tepeyac is above all things a mother figure. He will address her in terms that leave no doubt as to the reality of this identity. She is an object of aid and succour, a dispeller of doubts and anxieties. To her go men with problems. She is the recipient of petitions from the poor and the oppressed and of rewards for past help from the rich and successful. This is as true in Zamora as in any other Mexican community.

There can be little doubt that the Virgin of Guadalupe fills a very real need in the emotional life of the adult male. The tendency to remain bound to the mother is expressed in a variety of ways. In a number of life histories collected in Zamora, the mother is depicted as loving and understanding, an intermediary between a son and his father. The Virgin of Guadalupe functions in essentially the same way, except that she is a heavenly mother. TAT responses also support the hypothesis of a strong mother fixation on the part of *zamorano* males. Card 6 BM of the Murray TAT shows an elderly woman standing with her back to a young man. Seventy-nine percent of the respondents identify the woman as "mother" and the young man as "son." Typically, the son is perceived as being in some kind of trouble or burdened by a great problem, while the mother is upset and either lectures her son or tries to give him helpful advice. The following are the most common thematic responses:

TABLE 2   CLASSIFICATION OF THEMATIC RESPONSES

Man	Theme in Percent of Stories	Woman	Theme in Percent of Stories
Identified as "son"	79	Identified as "mother"	79
Son in trouble	46	Mother sad, upset	39
Son repentant	18	Mother lectures, rebukes	29
Going on journey	14	Mother gives advice	14

In many stories, the son has done something wrong and is receiving a just reprimand from his mother:

This seems to be a picture with a mother and a son. Apparently she has been lecturing her son on something he has done. He looks ashamed and repentant. It appears that she is unhappy, her arms are crossed and perhaps she has been crying.

Or:

Here we have a suffering mother and her remorseful son. He is regretting the evil action which has caused unhappiness to his mother.

In a smaller number of instances, the son may simply bring a difficult problem to his mother:

> This gives the impression of a mother and a son. Both of them look worried, perhaps he has come to discuss some problem he has. The mother gives what opinion she can about whatever they are dealing with. The young man looks very downhearted . . . and the mother is trying to do what she can to help him.

Or:

> A good man getting advice from his mother. He is probably thinking of marriage and awaiting the solution which his mother will give him.

These are, of course, male responses, but they point to the special veneration—it is little short of this—which the society has for motherhood. Not only do adult *zamoranos* pay special tribute to their mothers, but the mother role is given cultural recognition in various other ways. Mothers' Day (*dia de la madre*) is made the occasion for family celebrations and the town boasts a statue dedicated to *la madre*, "the mother." Women in general may be ambivalent creatures, but mothers carry only positive connotations. If they punish or rebuke, there is no question that this chastisement is perfectly justified.

"VERGÜENZA": AN IDEAL WOMANLY ATTRIBUTE

If one were to isolate the prime attribute demanded of a woman in Zamora, it would be that combination of modesty and shame that goes by the name of *vergüenza*. *Vergüenza* is usually translated in English as "shame"; shame in the sense that we refer to someone who lacks it as "shameless." *Vergüenza* encompasses shades of meaning which are not all applicable to feminine behavior. Thus a man who acts dishonorably is termed a *sinvergüenza* ("shameless"), and the term may also be used with reference to a criminal, a cheat, or even a coarse person.

Zamoranos see *vergüenza* as very much the product of upbringing—it has to be learned. Very young children are jokingly referred to as *sinvergüenzas*, for it is understood that they are too young to have learned the full meaning of shame. However, an older child is expected to behave properly; he should not be "forward" in the presence of adults and strangers, and in general treat adults with due respect. Behavior towards parents, especially proper respect for the father, is influenced by feelings of shame. Young men of the upper and middle class, sometimes even *campesino* youths, will not smoke in front of their fathers, for shame would make them uncomfortable.

For women, shame early takes on some clearly sexual attributes. Anything which casts doubt on a woman's virtue is an attack on her *vergüenza*. Before marriage, the obvious minimal requirement is virginity—to have lost the one is a clear indication of the loss of the other. According to the same formula, the culture insists on total marital fidelity for the woman. But "sexual" should be interpreted very broadly. Thus, a woman who dresses at all provocatively makes available to a wide audience of males something that by right belongs to her husband alone. As a case in point, in Zamora it is still very daring for girls and women to swim in mixed company. In nearby Jacona, a spa has a number of small walled-in swimming pools for family groups, while another spa in the same town features "women only" days. Even very young girls are taught to sit in a modest manner, for otherwise, it is said, how will they learn to feel *vergüenza*? Correct feminine behavior also requires great care in the choice of friends and associates. A woman should be careful not to find herself alone in the company of an adult male other than a member of her family, and even married women seldom visit singly or go shopping by themselves.

Age provides some relief from the heavy burdens of *vergüenza*. Old women may associate more freely, for they no longer have to fear suspicions regarding their virtue. There are cultural forms that seem to signal this changed condition. The dress of the elderly woman—one is almost tempted to say the habit—is a shapeless black garment and a matching black shawl (*rebozo*). There is nothing elegant, nothing flattering, about this uniform. Its manifest function is mourning, but while younger women mourn only for a limited time, two years at the most for a close family member, beyond middle age, mourning once put on is never taken off. Dressed in this manner, a woman can go abroad in the knowledge that no male eye will follow her. Her dress proclaims her position, and not surprisingly, there is little difference between the dress of the mourning woman and the habit of the nun. In a sense, both are sexless.

COURTSHIP AND MARRIAGE

For the woman, marriage is a shift in authority. Before marriage she is under the control of her parents; after marriage responsibility for her actions and behavior devolve on her husband. There is a change in masters, but no great change in freedom of action, at least ideally. My impression is that some married women of the middle and upper classes exercise considerable authority within the family circle, especially in middle age. However, the culture does stress that the role of the woman is subordinate. This subordination is validated by references to natural law: Women were created to fill a subordinate position and men were granted mastery.

The sexual aspects of marriage, apart from procreation and motherhood, are assumed to be relatively unimportant for women. Satisfaction and fulfillment are supposed to be derived from bearing children, and many *zamoranos* will quite frankly say that women do not enjoy sex but simply resign themselves to it as a duty. This viewpoint is perhaps understandable when it is remembered that for the man the sexual aspects of marriage are viewed as a form of conquest. The man takes what is his due; the woman submits to rightful demands. How women feel is more problematic, but to the extent that such a delicate subject can be broached, my wife received the very definite impression that most well-to-do *zamoranas* considered sex as a rather nasty male imposition.

This fits in with what we know of sexual education, or rather, the lack of it. Typically, middle- and upper-class women contract matrimony quite uninitiated in matters of sex. According to a medical informant, ignorance of the relationship between intercourse and procreation is not unusual, enlightenment (in the form of maternal instruction) coming only in the course of the first pregancy. While one may doubt that women are quite as ignorant as they are portrayed to be, or say they are, sex must nevertheless be the locus for a multitude of fears, fantasies, and anxieties.

When a middle- or upper-class family decides it is time for a daughter to marry, a survey is made of available young men. As these young men must come from families of the same general social and economic station, the choice is often limited. The families of suitable *jovenes* (young men) are informed in various roundabout ways that the daughter of Señor so-and-so is of sufficient age to be courted. Those young men—or, better said, their families—who have some interest in the girl make this known to the family of the girl through several available informal channels, often an older woman known for her discretion.

The formal *noviazgo* (courtship) institution is not entered into without considerable deliberation. Selected young men are permitted the opportunity to see something of the girl in closely supervised situations, such as *fiestas* and family picnics. It is not expected that a girl should be engaged to or marry a total stranger, and in fact this does not occur.

The *noviazgo* is entered into after certain preliminary arrangements have been worked out. These arrangements are in part financial and include agreements on the size of the dowry and an assurance of the economic prospects of the would-be bridegroom. Only after these important questions have been settled, although not necessarily in all details, can the two young people enter into a formal engagement. Negotiations may be broken off without loss of dignity to either party at any stage prior to this point. Broken engagements are very rare.

In Zamora, adult female relatives, generally cousins or aunts, serve as the intermediaries of choice in arranging preliminary negotiations. They carry various proposals between the two families and function much like the go-betweens and marriage brokers encountered in some other societies. In Zamora, though, the role is not institutionalized and is covert rather than overt. The principals—that is, the male heads of the families—come together only after the groundwork has been laid; if negotiations should collapse prior to a formal announcement of engagement, the honor and dignity of the heads of the families remain intact. Until a formal understanding has been reached, and in some cases, a contract signed, all that has taken place may be lightly dismissed as the meddling of old women, and consequently, of little importance.

After the engagement, the young people, now referred to as *novios*, enjoy certain limited privileges. The girl remains heavily chaperoned, but the boy is allowed to visit at certain clearly specified times, although he is never permitted to come and go at will. The father of the *novia* defines the rules for meetings and the amount of time the *novios* may spend together. Typically, when a *novio* calls, the girl may see him only in the company of a well-trusted guardian of morality, generally an older female of the family, sometimes a long-established family retainer. Many fathers prohibit the *novio* all entry into the house so that the couple are forced to communicate either through the main entrance or, more often, via the *reja*, the barred window of some front room. The *novio* stands outside the street while the *novia* speaks to him through the wrought-iron barrier, her chaperon sitting discreetly a few paces behind her.

Young men may not like these harsh restrictions, but the rules are so taken for granted that few attempts are made to circumvent them. Many young men know that other modes of courtship exist, but there is little questioning of the local standards. Furthermore, parental control of girls is often rationalized as a protection for the *novio*, it shows that the girl has been well brought up, that her chastity has been protected.

It does not seem likely, however, that the system can be fully explained as a protective device. Loss of a daughter, in Zamora as in other societies, is a necessity that cannot be avoided. In the meantime, though, the path can be made as thorny as possible for the man who will ultimately claim her. Not only is the *novio* treated with extreme suspicion, but he is made to feel the indignities of his place. The father of an engaged daughter has it in his power to humble a person of similar station, albeit a young one, in a manner that would otherwise be quite intolerable. This is perhaps his greatest compensation for the loss involved.

Engagements are long in Zamora; two, three, or even more years are a normal span. First, a young man has to achieve enough financial self-sufficiency to support a wife in the approved style. In the middle and upper classes, the social components we are chiefly concerned with, this generally entails an apprenticeship in the family business which may last for three to five years after secondary school ends. Marriage before that time is quite out of the question.

Secondly, the older people of the community, that is, those in control, hold the belief that long betrothals are good in themselves. A girl is supposed to be more diligent and obedient if she has the prospects of a marriage before her. It is also said that a girl who reaches her late teens or early twenties without becoming engaged will be depressed, moody, and irritable. The assumption is that an unengaged girl must either suffer from personality defects, such as a very bad temper, or be unacceptable because of doubtful chastity, or be extremely ugly. Girls, therefore, do not resist engagement, but hope for it, and to the best of their limited ability, plan for it.

Engagement is also said to "improve" young men. A *novio* is likely to be well-behaved and "serious" (*serio*) if he knows that his actions and behavior may influence promotion within the family enterprise. Long engagements are thus a technique for controlling youth, and although few parents would describe the system in these terms, it certainly favors the tractability of the young. On the whole, the technique seems highly effective. Marriage, for both men and women, is the gateway to full adult status. The man by the fact of marriage shows that he is in a position to support a family and can take a responsible place in society. There is also the feeling that marriage is the natural state for adults and that there must be something radically wrong with the man who remains single. It has been hinted to me that unmarried adult men harbor some vice, are *viciosos*, a concept which covers a multitude of sins: Perhaps the individual in question drinks too much, is a homosexual, likes to run after women to an extent that becomes antisocial, or is simply irresponsible. Such suspicions, however unfounded, can prove harmful. Thus, a professional man in his middle thirties, a man who by all other standards is excellently trained and endowed, finds it very difficult to get clients. The fact that he is single is enough to blight his prospects.

For the woman, marriage is the moment for which she has been waiting for many years. For her it also signifies success and completion. Marriage promises a whole new set of plans and activities: household management, procreation, perhaps even some broadening of personal freedom. From both sides of the *reja*, if for different reasons, marriage seems to be a prize worth waiting for, especially since the culture offers no alternative avenues to adult status.

COURTSHIP AND MARRIAGE IN LOWER-CLASS SETTINGS

The patterns so far examined are applicable only to the upper and middle classes. Among *campesinos* marriage is entered into without long engagements and it is not at all uncommon for girls of fifteen or sixteen to wed boys two or three years their senior. In such unions, the economic aspects dwindle to insignificant proportions. Marriage contracts and formal dowry arrangements are unknown, although a girl will generally contribute something to the new household, perhaps linen or kitchen utensils, maybe some savings or a small present of money from her family. Even such small contributions to setting up the new household are not mandatory.

A boy is considered old enough for marriage as soon as he is capable of doing a man's work. In agricultural labor a boy of eighteen can work as well and as hard as a man of thirty, although he may lack some of the knowledge of the older man. But since physical labor is the *campesino*'s main economic asset, his chances of marriage in no way improve with the passage of time.

Ideally, standards of feminine chastity are as applicable to *campesino* girls as to those of the upper classes, and considering the young age of *campesino* and other lower-class wives, virginity is probably the norm. My impression, though, is that sex is much less of a burden for nonelite girls. Girls seem to marry with fewer fears, perhaps even with greater knowledge of what they are entering into. Especially in the small hamlets surrounding Zamora, sexuality seems to be something taken for granted. Families live in closely packed quarters, sometimes two or three related nuclear families sharing a house. Quite young girls help in household tasks, including the supervision of infants. Such household arrangements, which allow older married sisters to act as mentors for their younger unmarried siblings, plus observations from farmyard and field, apparently mitigate against marriage being the traumatic experience that it is for upper- and middle-class girls.

7 / The economy of the Zamora region

DELIMITING THE REGIONAL SPHERE

Throughout this report we have made reference to the Zamora region, that is to say, the town of Zamora, its satellite communities, and the surrounding countryside. For purposes of simplicity, we have equated the region with the *municipio*, the political subdivision of which Zamora is the administrative center. Although the *municipio* is more than an arbitrary administrative unit, corresponding as it does to some measure of physical, cultural, and economic integration, the boundaries of the local political jurisdiction do not fully represent the facts of economic reality.

As we have had occasion to mention, the town of Zamora is the second largest urban concentration in the state of Michoacán. Economically, this means that the "Zamora region" encompasses an area well beyond the *municipio* boundaries. Although it is difficult to delineate the area with great precision, Zamora is the center of an economic network tapping a hinterland of several hundred square miles. Roughly speaking, Zamora businessmen consider territory within one hundred kilometers (roughly sixty miles) of Zamora as forming part of *la region de Zamora*, although some operate further afield.

INDUSTRY

In and around the town of Zamora are a number of industrial enterprises, none of which can be counted as large and most of which are small, even dwarf, firms. The biggest plant employs 150 workers (plus sales and supervisory staff) and is still much larger than the average. A factory with thirty workers is considered an industry of consequence; many are smaller.

Virtually all Zamora firms are locally owned independent entities engaged in the processing of raw materials into market-ready products. Technologically, these are generally one-process operations needing minimal intrafactory industrial organization or cooperative ventures between separate firms.

In 1957–1958, the following plants were operating in Zamora or in nearby localities:

Cigarette factory
Sweater and knitted goods factory
Three flour mills
Three soft-drink bottling plants
Two alfalfa dehydrating plants
Animal feed plant
Tractor distributor and assembly plant for simple agricultural implements
Furniture factory
Tequila factory
Plant for the slaughter, processing, and freezing of poultry
Two tire retread and repair plants.

This list covers the nontraditional industries of recent origin. Apart from these, there are many small businesses which produce regional foods, tiles, candles, chocolates, bricks, and ice. They operate with a minimum of capital and the simplest technology. They derive most of their labor from within the family and operate on a day-to-day basis to meet local current needs. These industries can best be regarded as domestic enterprises and are seldom even of regional importance.

With reference to the listed industries, the most obvious characteristic is that they are almost wholly engaged in the processing of local agricultural produce. Exceptions to this rule are few. The sweater factory purchases most of its wool supplies in the national market; the cigarette factory (the largest plant in the area) obtains some of its leaf from the tobacco growing regions of the states of Nayarit and Veracruz, although it is making increasing use of company owned plantations in southern Michoacán; the soft-drink bottlers develop their product from syrups and concentrates produced outside the region.

On the otherhand, the agricultural produce processed in the Zamora plants comes chiefly from the valley of Zamora and other communities within easy trucking distance from the town. Just as the sources of raw material are chiefly regional, so is the market for finished products, though somewhat less so. The knitted goods made in the Zamora sweater factory are sold throughout the Mexican *altiplano* and the northern states of the Republic. The cigarette factory distributes its brands in five states of northwestern Mexico. Other firms concentrate on more localized markets. Thus, of the three soft-drink plants, one has the Michoacán franchise for a nationally and internationally known brand of beverages; another distributes a product known only in Zamora and nearby villages; while the third, something of an exception in the Zamora scene, is situated in the neighboring *municipio* of Jacona and is owned and controlled by a large international corporation. The flour mills and dehydrating plants also ship some of their production outside the area, although the regional market is said to be the most important.

While the market for processed goods is thus more extensive than the region from which the raw materials are derived, manufacturers tend to agree that competition and organizational problems greatly increase with distance. Distance itself, however, is only one of the factors operating to maintain a regional market orientation. Shippers and manufacturers do state that distance increases transportation costs, but more than this, the system of purchase and market arrangements favored by Zamora entrepreneurs places a premium on personal ties and individual ar-

Manager of feed plant (right) and factory workforce. The size of the plant is typical of industrial enterprises in 1958.

rangements, and such networks work best in the regional context. Most producers, therefore, concentrate on maintaining regional sales rather than on increasing their market by going further afield. Entrepreneurs complain that outside the region few people know them (and hence it is difficult to do business); that for the same reason the police and other authorities demand exorbitant bribes; and, of course, competition is keener.

The difficulties encountered by a poultry processing firm demonstrates the dangers of the extraregional world as seen by Zamora entrepreneurs. As there is little local demand for frozen poultry in the region, most of it is sold to supermarkets in Mexico City. To begin with, in order to obtain permission for such sales in the Federal District, it was necessary to arrange an interview with a high government official. But the permit obtained only guaranteed the right of sale. As the owner explained:

Everywhere you go it is the same, one has to bribe for everything. . . . Every truck which I send to Mexico [City] must bribe cops on the road; five pesos for this one, ten pesos for the other, it all adds to cost. . . . The customer pays the higher prices, I get lower profits, Mexico suffers. In this country you can't do a thing without having to pay somebody for the right of doing it.

Experiences of this nature no doubt reinforce the timidity of Zamora entrepreneurs. Many are of the opinion that crooked politicians and large national and foreign corporations are in league to stifle the small producer, or at least make expansion difficult for him. As one Zamora businessman put it:

When it comes to one of the big businesses, the small official is careful not to make trouble, for he knows that important men in government invest their money in such enterprises. Also, the big corporations have another advantage: should they have to bribe a powerful government official, they are in a much better financial position to do so.

These opinions may not faithfully reflect reality. No doubt, they are in part rationalizations for timid economic behavior, but they are also commonly held beliefs and as such guide business policies. To move outside the regional market is to give up the known and safe for the unknown and dangerous, to exchange a position of relative power for one of relative insignificance. Some Zamora entrepreneurs have attempted to enter into the national market, but I know of only two who have pinned their hopes on this type of expansion. Most show a distinct preference for launching another business enterprise to utilize a further sector of the safe regional market.

RETAILING

The town of Zamora has for generations been an important market center. The same lines of communication that permit *zamorano* businessmen to tap the surrounding countryside for raw materials bring agricultural produce to the city markets, customers to the local stores, and shipments of various staples to the merchants and brokers of the *cabecera*. This fairly complex movement of goods and customers must be analyzed in some detail, for trade and distribution operate at various levels and involve different commodities. The trading networks centered on Zamora antedate the industrial development of the town and the establishment of modern means of communication. Even peasants who are largely subsistence oriented must acquire a minimum of manufactured goods and processed articles, even if these are no more than the occasional *machete*, needles, *manta* cloth, and hardware items. The *municipio* has long lived in a money economy, although the funds available to its poorer members are restricted. Then again, Zamora as a trading center caters not only to *municipio* needs but to customers from many outlying communities.

To pay for these necessities, the peasant must either find some way of transforming his surpluses into cash or exchange them for the goods required. Direct barter, while not unknown, seems to account for only a fraction of the petty trade.

Tarascan Indian women selling fruit, pottery, and song birds.

Mestizo *market vendors and hardware items.*

Tarascan woman and mestizo *laborer (he holds a tumpline for carrying loads) discussing the price of avocados.*

Peasants will sell at the municipal market, and more rarely engage in door-to-door hawking. This takes care of small lots—milk from the family cow, the basket of corn, and so forth. When more substantial quantities are involved, the peasant will typically sell to a middleman, one of the Zamora merchants with whom he has a trading arrangement. In most cases this is an established relationship: The merchant advances goods or money to the peasant in time of need and in exchange purchases his crops at harvest time, deducting loans and other favors. We will examine such relationships in more detail when we look into the organization of agriculture.

A multitude of vendors, pedlars, and small shopkeepers supply the demands of the peasants and the poor. Often this is small-scale trade in the most literal sense, for the units sold can be the smallest that a particular product can be broken down into: the single cigarette, a few inches of ribbon, enough plastic sheeting to cover a hole in the roof or a crack in the window. Many of these petty traders have their place of business in the same markets where the countrymen bring their produce. Others roam the square in front of the cathedral with trays of cheap trinkets, lengths of cloth, or outstretched arms displaying straw hats or nylon underwear. Of somewhat greater substance are the proprietors of the little stores in the back streets of the poorer sections of town. Their clientele is much the same—visiting peasants and the lower class—and their merchandising methods are of a similar order.

The Zamora markets, and many of the small stores too, are open seven days a week, but the weekend, especially Sunday, brings an influx of *campesinos* from the country. The trip to town is also something of an outing, a time to treat the children to soft drinks, eat hot barbecued meat at the market stalls, or roam around the center of town looking at the displays of expensive clothes and shining appliances in the windows of the big stores. This is also the time of the week one notices a fairly high proportion of Tarascan men and women, behaving much like *campe-*

sinos, but in a more restrained manner. The *municipio* does its part in making the occasion a festive one by providing band concerts in the plaza. The Zamora soccer team plays on Sunday afternoon and many visitors stay to swell the crowd of local spectators.

Turning from the peasant and lower-class customer to the petty trader, the step from ambulatory trade and market stall vending to the acquisition of a permanent store, however small and poorly supplied, represents a major discontinuity in economic pursuits. Some of the retailers who sell in the market are businessmen of some capital, owners of trucks who buy their wares from major wholesalers in the large cities and sell them in many villages and small towns. These appear only periodically in Zamora, perhaps to dispose of a load of blankets or a shipment of kitchen utensils. Most vendors, though, are local people with a reduced stock-in-trade.

The man or woman who brings a weekly basket of produce to market or sells items around the street does not for these reasons cease to be a peasant, although not all who engage in this kind of trade are peasants. But for what we may call the part-time peasant-trader, the commitment to trade is only partial, a marginal activity that may bring in a few extra pesos, but is of secondary importance compared to agriculture. Just as the profits from such ventures are necessarily small, so are the risks. Overheads are reduced to insignificant proportions; the value of the stock is measured in tens rather than in hundreds of pesos.

But the difference between the vendor and the small storekeeper is to be reckoned in more than monetary terms. The investment of the small storekeeper is generally greater than that of the vendor, but what is perhaps more important, he depends on his trade as the primary means of livelihood. If the business does not go according to plan, the small storekeeper cannot easily pack up and devote all his energies to working the land. Conversely, there are few set limits on the expansion of his business. If successful, he may graduate from a hole-in-the-wall *tienda* (store) or a permanent booth in the town square arcades to a large and more substantial establishment, ultimately even to the ownership of a major store in the center of town.

This evolution can be followed in a number of specific instances, but the initial step is seldom taken without a good deal of deliberation. The world of the city and permanent trade is for the most part alien to the *campesino*. It lacks the simple direct relationship between effort and sustenance, the property of partial control (in bad times the family can more or less feed itself from the land it works) that the *campesino* feels he exercises over his future. This attitude is illustrated in the reply of an *ejidatario* to the query on whether he had ever contemplated setting up a store in Zamora:

> My wife has often urged me to leave the *ejido* and settle in Zamora. As a man who can read and write I should have no difficulty with accounts. Furthermore, I speak English [the informant had spent a number of years in the United States as a *bracero* and spoke English quite well] and might be able to make some *centavos* from the tourists. But here in the country nobody bothers me, no policemen, no inspectors. Life in the city is much harder, you have to compete with the wealthy merchants, be on the right side of the authorities. There is also

something else. I like living surrounded by my crops, while the thought of being cooped up in a small street depresses me. I'm afraid my wife will have to resign herself to her clay oven and to cooking with charcoal.

A series of gradations link small retailing geared to the demands of *campesinos* and the poor in general to the larger stores catering to the trade of the middle and upper classes. Some of the major stores in town are clearly outlets of a specialized type (furniture and appliance stores, clothing stores, and so on), but the typical Zamora store continues to be the *miscelánea*, a general store, that attempts to meet a broad range of customer requirements. On its shelves may be found a medley of goods, everything from cosmetics to carborundum stones.

In a manner not unlike the operations in the market, even in the larger stores the units retailed tend to be small. Ordinary typing paper, to take one example, is not sold by the box but in bunches of five or ten sheets, or even individually (I have seen well-dressed, and obviously rich, customers buying one envelope and two sheets of paper). If the customer buys in bulk (a whole package of envelopes, a case of beer) he expects to be granted a discount.

The main difference between middle- and upper-class stores and lower-class ones lies in the range and quality of the merchandise. Stores that cater to the lower classes stock a very restricted sample, often no more than three or four shelves of groceries—lard, a few tinned goods, dry beans, cheap *aguardiente* (cane liquor), some candies, and the ever-present soft drinks. At the other end of the scale it is possible to purchase such delicacies as Scotch whisky (120 pesos a bottle, about 10 dollars) and imported Strasbourg *pâté de fois gras*.

Zamora business practices and customer attitudes would strike the North American observer as very conservative. Although the range of goods in the major stores is quite extensive, little need seems to be felt by store owners to move the merchandise rapidly. There are no sales or similar incentives, and inventories are not changed to meet shifts in consumption or to stimulate the buying of new products. A particular line will be kept in stock until it has been sold out, and only then will the proprietor acquire newer or more successful models.

In part, such sales policies are possible because the average Zamora customer has not been sensitized to minute variations in the product. Many articles continue to be sold generically rather than by brand name. Butter is not a cube enveloped in a distinctive wrapper, but something brought into town once a week by a peasant from the hills; a refrigerator is not appraised as being newer or older, but simply as a refrigerator.

In time Zamora customers will no doubt become increasingly aware of the supposed advantages of new products. The region is not immune to the style setting forces of magazines, radio, and television. But so far, the inroads made by nationally advertised products, particularly food and household items, are relatively few. It is not so much that brand names are unobtainable in Zamora, but that they constitute a small percentage of the articles purchased. However, some customer shifts are observable, and these may be indicative of the shape of things to come. During the year of our stay (1957–1958), an enterprising Guadalajara bakery had managed to penetrate the Zamora market with a popular brand of nationally advertised sliced white bread and the local bakers were complaining of the competition. One reason for the success of this product lies in the fact that it is identified as an item of middle-class consumption, but is still within the reach of most pockets.

On the whole, though, Zamora housewives are prejudiced against packaged foods. Processed foods are thought to be both unhealthy and the recourse of the incompetent cook. In the popular folklore, the gastric ailments suffered by foreigners are attributed to "bad eating," and in Zamora opinion, North American cuisine is pretty much equated with the opening of cans and the mixing of powders.

PEASANT LIFE AND LABOR

Although small-scale industrialization has made substantial headway in the course of the last three or four decades, the Zamora region is still fundamentally agricultural, particularly with respect to employment. Even if we limit ourselves to the *municipio* proper—the area of greatest industrial activity—some fifty percent of the labor force makes its living from the land.

The bulk of Zamora farmers are peasant agriculturalists working a few hectares of land. Part of this land grows crops for home consumption and part is devoted to cash crops. The ratio of cash crops to consumption crops is determined by a number of factors including prices and such marketing arrangements as the farmer may work out with wealthy merchants and brokers.

The category of small farmers includes the *ejidatarios* and the small number of *campesinos* who work their own privately owned smallholdings. At the other end of the scale, some twenty percent of the land is divided into fairly large farms, none over 100 hectares, geared primarily to market production. The two scales represent differences in farm size and also in economic organization and technology.

Before we examine these two agricultural systems, it is necessary to say something about the relationship of production costs with both crops (cash or subsistence) and the quality of land. In simple terms, high quality land is more expensive to work than poor land and cash crops tend to be more expensive to grow than subsistence crops. Obviously no one would be foolish enough to risk a lot of money in raising crops on marginal land, crops that can be wiped out in one heavy downpour. Typically, then, marginal land is worked with the minimum of capital investment, although the human effort may still be heavy. Such capital as the farmer has (for the renting of machinery, the purchase of quality seed, fertilizers, insecticides, and so forth is earmarked for irrigated and humid lands.

Similarly, market crops must generally meet certain standards of quality and thus require more care and effort, not to mention the fact that growing of cash crops generally entails the purchase of expensive seed. Compensation for the higher investment in time and money comes in the form of higher profits, but before these profits can be realized it is necessary to procure the capital. However, capital for small farmers is in short supply, and the lack of it helps to account for the relatively poor showing of small-scale and *ejido* agriculture compared to the higher outputs of larger and more heavily capitalized farms.

It is not surprising, therefore, that the major concern of *ejidatarios* is the shortage of capital. In discussing this and related matters with them, very few *ejidatarios* felt that technology was a major stumbling block to higher production: They worked with what technology they could afford and were perfectly willing to innovate technologically if the opportunity presented itself. Not a few, in fact, contrasted their experience with farm machinery in the United States with the archaic technology which poverty often compels them to use on their land.

In many instances, this shortage of capital forces the small farmer to establish a patronage relationship with some man of means, generally a well-to-do farmer or *cabecera* merchant. The system has been described to me by one *ejidatario* as

Campesino *in town to sell turkeys. Small store carries shoes and boots and is patronized by peasants and poor townsmen.*

"the only way one can afford to grow good crops. I provide the land and the labor, while Sr. _____ makes available the money, seed, fertilizer, and similar necessities," while another stated more bluntly that "we really have no choice in the matter since the banks won't lend us any money." Although the *ejidatario* has title to the land, the system is essentially one of sharecropping. In not a few cases, it is the man with money, and not the small farmer, who decides what crops will be grown, and the phenomenon of the *ejidatario* leasing his land to a wealthy man and then working for him as a hired laborer is not unknown.

This lack of capital does much to explain the popularity of migratory labor in the United States. It is, in fact, often the only way that the small farmer can afford to operate his farm with some degree of independence. *Ejidatarios*, as well as small independent farmers, also hire themselves out to bigger operators, but such work is poorly paid and consequently much less attractive.

There are also, of course, many *campesinos* without land, and for these men the choices are even more limited. The standard of living of the local *campesinos* may not be the lowest in Mexico, but for those without land it is not much above subsistence. Minimum wages for agricultural work in the *municipio* are 8.50 pesos a day (1957) and perhaps as much as 10 pesos can be earned during harvest time. According to my own calculations, it is impossible to see how a family of four (husband, wife, two young children) can live on anything less than 15 pesos a day, and even this calls for a very reduced and unbalanced diet.

Food consumption relies heavily on two items, corn, which is eaten mostly in the form of *tortillas*, and beans. Milk, meat, fresh vegetables, fruits, and fats are eaten irregularly and sporadically. Meat in particular is a luxury item, something reserved for festive occasions. I remember a three- or four-year-old boy, the son of a quite successful *ejidatario*, begging his father to buy him a *chivito*, a small goat. I asked the child whether he wanted it as a pet. "Oh no," he answered, "I'll fatten him up and then we can all eat meat." On the basis of this far from ideal diet the *campesino* must find strength to cultivate his fields or hire out as agricultural labor.

With the exception of a few peak months, underemployment, if not outright unemployment, is the lot of many *campesinos*. It is even possible, as some peasants maintain, that the employment situation is worse today than it was before the Revolution. The old *hacienda* organization was based on a resident labor force. As plantation workers, *peones* might hope for, if not exactly be able to rely upon, a small amount of year-round aid from the *hacendados* for whom they worked. Today, in an era of "free labor," a growing number of landless peasants must take their chances in a saturated open market or find work elsewhere.

The really depressed segment of the rural population is made up of those peasants not fortunate enough to have acquired or inherited *ejido* lands. This landless group increases as more *ejidos* are transferred from the first to the second generation. Legally at least, an *ejidatario* can pass on title to the land to only one of his offspring, and although not a few allotments are now worked by groups of brothers or other family combinations (one individual holding legal title), every passing year puts extra pressure on the land.

In discussing the *ejido* system, many observers fail to understand that although it has benefited the peasant, especially in its initial phases, a number of advantages have also accrued to the private landowner. First and most obviously, the parcelling of land into *ejidos*, which took place on a nation-wide scale, withdrew many hectares from commercial production and thus increased the value of the crops grown on private land. As we noted earlier, the value of land in *pequeñas pro- piedades* did not automatically rise, owing to fears of further expropriation. It was in fact possible to buy land cheaply during the early agrarian reform period, and much Zamora property changed hands at this time.

The establishment of *ejidos* disrupted the archaic system of *hacienda* organization. *Campesinos* either received *ejido* holdings or were forced on the open labor market. These changes brought about a drastic restructuring of residence and settlement patterns and altered the relationships between farm worker and employer. No longer did *campesinos*, or at least the majority of them, have their homes on the land of their employers. Those not lucky enough to receive *parcelas* were transformed into rural wage earners working for a fixed period of time determined by the needs of the landowner.

It is conceivable that wage labor might have worked in favor of landless *campesinos* if they had been organized for some form of collective action. This, at least in Zamora, was not the case. The only group with some degree of com- munal organization, the *ejidatarios*, were more concerned with their own holdings than with leading or participating in some kind of united action. Not without truth is the statement of an observant Zamora businessman that agrarian reform "tamed the Zapatistas"—the peasant militants. Landless workers had to be satisfied with whatever protection, and it was little enough, afforded by the minimum wage legislation. It is not easy to evaluate the changes that have occurred in the standard of living of the poorest peasants over the last twenty or thirty years, but what is not in doubt is that most landless *campesinos* believe that real wages are lower now than they were in the late nineteen thirties and during the Second World War.

THE ORGANIZATION OF "PEQUEÑAS PROPIEDADES"

The *pequeñas propiedades* of the region are chiefly devoted to the production of cash crops. A good proportion of this output is sold locally to merchants and brokers and to the operators of mills and plants. Many of the larger landowners are able to process at least part of their yield in facilities which they either own out- right, or, as is more common, in which they have some financial stake as one of a number of partners. Those *propietarios* who are not at the same time industrialists can generally count on some other capital-producing enterprise besides farming. Some are merchants, others are businessmen or professionals. Thus, unlike the *ejidatarios* and the small independent peasant farmers, commercial farmers are much better able to withstand temporary setbacks. Furthermore, since they are men of some means—sometimes very wealthy—they find it much easier to raise capital.

The typical owner of a rural property, other than the small peasant farmer, finds it possible to operate his estate as a fairly profitable venture. Farming for money rather than for food, he may devote all his land to whatever crop or combination of crops is judged to be the most remunerative for a given market situation. The area under cultivation is generally large enough to permit the use of fairly sophisticated techniques of cultivation, including some mechanization.

We do not imply that all the landowners of the area make the best possible use of their land and resources. Perhaps the majority are content to operate at less than maximum efficiency, but even farms that are not very well run seem to make a profit. My notes contain a description of what I judged to be a poorly run farm and I include it as a necessary corrective to the overly simplistic dichotomy that is sometimes made between "traditional" peasant agriculture and "progressive" market-oriented farming.

> The farm is not clean—the owner himself describes it as a "pigsty"—and gives the impression of being poorly run. The place is covered with flies. Nevertheless, the owner is very proud of the fact that it is one of the largest farms in the region.

> Around the farm there seem to be a great number of unproductive hangers-on, including half a dozen teen-age boys who spend most of their time smoking and telling stories. Leisure is occasionally punctuated with much giving of orders— "Let the chickens out for air"; "Make sure the bags of fertilizer don't get wet"; "Fill in those holes with earth"—but no one seems to have a standard task and new work groups must be organized to meet every contingency.

The proprietor of this farm is the same individual who on another occasion asked me whether 100,000 pesos would be enough for a projected trip to Europe.

The major distributor of agricultural machinery in Zamora maintains that there are "two distinct groups of agriculturalists" in the region, "the old farmers and the new farmers who use old methods" and "the old and new agriculturalists who use new methods." The first group consists of people

> who with only great difficulty adapt themselves to mechanization. There is an erroneous belief among such people that tractors should be used only for plowing and harrowing. I maintain that these tasks constitute but 40 percent of the efficiency or possibilities of the tractor. These people continue to utilize teams of mules or oxen for seeding and for other necessary tasks of cultivation.

> The other agriculturalists are the ones who do everything possible to use their machinery for highest performance. They are also the ones who are most interested in using new systems of pest control, better seeds, better fertilizers, and so on.

> Many of those who rely so much on antiquated methods do not do so for lack of money, for sometimes they could well afford the new techniques.

In my own observation, the most efficient *pequeños propietarios* are men who are not full-time farmers but have other interests and businesses. Some are men of *campesino* background, others are urbanites rather than countrymen. What they have in common is a breath of interest and experience.

Taken as a group, there is little doubt that the average private owner is a more efficient operator than the average *ejidatario* or smallholder. But for the most part, they are also men of limited education, at least in the formal sense of the word, and consequently make little use of technical literature having to do with agriculture. For instance, one cannot help noticing the absence in their homes of treatises on farming, magazines devoted to farm management, and so forth Nevertheless, they take a fairly pragmatic approach to farming, and if they learn that a technique or crop promises to make more money for them, especially if the risks are not too great, they are likely to give it a try.

Consequently, such new developments (for this area) as the cultivation of potatoes and strawberries, use of imported seeds, application of chemical fertilizers, soil tests, pest control measures, and mechanization have all originated on private estates. A few *ejidatarios* have managed to follow suit, but generally later, necessarily on a smaller scale, and often less successfully. A man with substantial holdings in the area was no doubt correct when he expressed the opinion that:

> The agriculture of the area has made many advances in the past twenty or thirty years. Today we use crops and utilize methods that were unknown in this area at the time of our fathers. But who has made these strides? Look around, ask questions. You will soon realize that every new development has been initiated by the owners of *pequeñas propiedades*.

This observation may be true enough, but fails to take into account factors like the size of *ejido* holdings which limit the use of modern technology and the difficulties which *ejidatarios* face in procuring loans and other assistance.

We have looked at the influences and resources, the methods, and aims, of the *pequeños propietarios* of the Zamora region. One further aspect merits consideration: these men are mostly individuals with an intimate knowledge of farming. Even those *propietarios* who are at the same time important industrialists of Zamora merchants—including a number who would fall into the category of *ricos*—first began as farmers. Some are progressive while others are substantially less so, but in either case agriculture is not a new experience. In the background of most of the leading men of Zamora is a peasant past, often in their own lifetimes, and seldom more than one generation removed.

Such men speak of farming as a "satisfying occupation." Sentences like "It is a pleasure to concern myself with the workings of the farm," or "I feel content to visit the *rancho*; my wife and children also enjoy it," constantly crop up in their conversation. A good deal has been written about whether peasants in fact feel a deep attachment to the land. It appears that these positive feelings are by no means a constant but rather are culturally specific—peasants in some areas and countries have a distinct dislike for their hard life and an antipathy to the land and all that has to do with it; others, in contrast, see the life of the farmer in a much more favorable light. With respect to Zamora, both peasants and *propietarios* evidence a highly positive emotional commitment. I have driven through farmland with an *ejidatario* passenger and been asked to stop to look at the "beautiful young corn," and while all kinds of complaints have been voiced—against *patrones* who ask too much, banks that lend too little, and merchants who do not pay enough— no one in my experience has ever denigrated the land per se. Life may be hard and could be much improved, but there are very few willing to exchange the life of the farmer for some other form of livelihood. Even the poorest peasant who owns a little land believes that he enjoys a measure of "independence," questionable though this assumption may be.

This esteem for the land may account for the degree of personal control exercised by *propietarios* in the running of their estates. Personal supervision is a feature of all business in Zamora, but it may indicate a transference of agricultural practice to other business fields. Although most independent farmers of means reside in the *cabecera*, the majority visit their farms several times a week, in some cases every day. This on-the-spot supervision contrasts sharply with the long absences and indirect control typical of the *hacienda* owners of prerevolutionary times.

THE PAST AND THE PRESENT

Zamoranos—including *ejidatarios*—tend to agree that contemporary private holdings are more efficient and more productive than the *haciendas* of forty or fifty years ago. They also concur that agriculture, in all its facets, would not have evolved as it has without the impetus of the Revolution. Interestingly enough, this opinion is shared by even the most wealthy men of the *municipio*. "The Revolution made it necessary for us to work our land properly," commented a *propietario*; "You would not believe how backward this region used to be," stated another. Few, therefore, regret the passing of the *hacienda* and the end of *hacendado* control: The *ejidatarios* know well where their *ejidos* came from; the *pequeños propietarios* fully realize that the Revolution and its aftermath permitted them to acquire land and position which otherwise would have been denied to them.

But beyond this antipathy for the old landowners and their system, there is a wide range of disagreement. Many *ejidatarios* and peasants without land would like to see *ejido* tenure extended to incorporate the remaining estates in private hands. Not that this alone would solve all their problems. Apart from the perennial credit difficulties, the small farmer complains that the *ejido* has not lived up to its promise. Much land may have been distributed, but real economic power still rests in the hands of the rich. They also complain of abandonment by a government ("The capital has abandoned the *campesinos*," is a cry that I have often heard) that has lost touch with the rural masses.

The private owners for their part take considerable pleasure in pointing out the shortcomings of *ejido* agriculture. The trouble, they say, is that the *ejido* is an "old-fashioned solution to Mexico's agricultural problems." It is granted that agrarian reform has kept the countryside peaceful, but only at the cost of crippling the rural economy. A further reason for dissatisfaction is the government policy of pegging the price of staples, especially corn, in order to "subsidize" the workers in urban factories. In fact, *propietarios* react in much the same way as *ejidatarios* to what they regard as discrimination in favor of the large industrial centers.

Propietarios are not slow to offer solutions aimed at revitalizing Mexican agriculture. Very few believe that it is either feasible or prudent to directly separate the *ejidatarios* from their land. The approach is more subtle. Many voice the opinion that it would be to the advantage of all concerned if *ejidatarios* were given full title to their land in order that they might engage in "normal business transactions," a euphemism that barely hides the assurance that in no time at all the *ejidatarios* would be forced or lured into selling their hectares. One farmer went so far as to specify the hoped for changes in considerable detail:

> The government is always talking about industrializing Mexico. But for industry you need people in the factories. If the *ejidatarios* were given the land they now control, many would find it profitable to sell their holdings to those able to make better use of them. In this way the land would be well-worked, it would produce plenty of food for Mexico, and many who are now *campesinos* would move to the cities. I believe that with the abundance resulting from good agricultural methods an increased urban population could easily be provided for. Everyone would be happy: workers well-fed in the factories; productive farms in the country.

This "solution" cannot of course be taken seriously. One thing the Mexican economy does not lack is an overabundance of unskilled hands, and any increase in the influx of peasants moving into the cities would only lower the already marginal existence of the urban poor. In all probability, Mexico will long continue to be a country with what is sometimes referred to as a "dual economy": a modern industrial sector located mainly in the larger cities coexisting with archaic forms of production (and related patronage relationships) in the countryside. The larger private farmers to some extent form part of both economic worlds.

8 / Entrepreneurial activity in Zamora

THE SOCIAL ORIGINS OF ENTREPRENEURS

In our discussion of the class structure of the *municipio* we have had occasion to comment on the origins and background of the present-day elite. Since changes in the economic sphere, in particular the growth and development of a regional industrial base, constitute the major discontinuity between prerevolutionary and contemporary (1958) Zamora, it would seem worthwhile to examine in more detail the major agents of change, especially the class of entrepreneurs that make up the core of the group we have referred to as the *ricos*.

Although not all *zamoranos* are in agreement on which individuals should or should not be numbered among the *ricos*, it proved easy enough to select a number of prominent men to whom all informants attribute elite status. The sample in question is made up of thirteen *zamoranos*, ten of whom are primarily industrialists and three whose chief interests lie in agriculture. Of the ten *industriales*, five founded the business themselves; three inherited the business from their fathers; one inherited the business from his father, who in turn had interited from his father; and one obtained full control of the business on the death of his brother, who had originally established the firm.

These figures show how recent industrialization is in Zamora. In only one instance does it have a depth of three generations, while the predominant pattern is that of the owner-founder. But industrial entrepreneurship is not only new, it is derived from rather unexpected social origins. Of the five owner-founders, three give their father's occupation as *agricultor* or *campesino*, one is the son of a small shopkeeper, the other the son of an engineer. At least three of the remaining industrialists—those who inherited rather than founded businesses—come ultimately from peasant backgrounds. Sixty percent of the sample group has direct links to the peasantry.

These would appear to be significant findings, findings at variance with what might be expected in terms of developmental theory. Thus, students of early industrialization in Europe and the United States have often noted the importance of craftsmen and mechanics as innovators and founders of industrial enterprises. There is an assumption that technical knowledge, often coupled with an urban background, gave such men significant advantages in the formative period of the Industrial Revolution. In Zamora, the situation is radically different Only one entrepreneur—a man who spent his early working life in an industrial city and then migrated to Zamora—would fit this pattern.

Given the antecedents of Zamora entrepreneurs, it comes as no surprise to find that the majority enjoyed little in the way of formal education. Of the total (both owner-founders and inheritors) six did not progress beyond primary school level, three had some sort of secondary or vocational education, while only one can be regarded as the product of higher education, and that not a university but a Catholic seminary. Even these figures do not tell the whole story. For most entrepreneurs education was mediocre and sporadic, and one man went as far as to confess that he had achieved functional literacy only in his twenties with the help of his wife.

Keeping in mind the antecedents of such men, very few of whom came from middle-class backgrounds, and not a single one from the cosmopolitan *hacendado* class, there is nothing extraordinary in such levels of formal education. Half a century ago the *campesino* who could write his name and read a simple text was still very much the exception. Also, and the value given to *cultura* to the contrary, it would seem that even those fathers who could have afforded a better education for their sons often chose not to do so. "My family was sufficiently well off," said one *rico* informant, "to have paid for a better education. But education beyond high school was thought of as a luxury, and anyhow I was needed at home to help my father."

The three upper-class *ricos* whose interests are primarily agricultural are also, and perhaps less surprisingly, predominantly of peasant stock. Two are the off-spring of *campesinos*, while the third is the son of a *hacendado* which, incidentally, makes him the only wealthy man in Zamora with links to the porfirian aristocracy. In contrast, peasant backgrounds are far less typical of the smaller businessmen of the *cabecera*. In a sample of fifteen such individuals (merchants, contractors, hotel proprietors, and so forth), nine indicated nonpeasant antecedents. An examination of life histories shows that most of those who are presently engaged in trade and commerce (other than *ricos* who may also have interests in these fields) are the contemporary representatives of the prerevolutionary middle class.

PRECONDITIONS FOR CHANGE

The rise of the Zamora *ricos* to a position of economic control and social and political influence is a singularly local phenomenon. It was this fact which was primarily responsible for my decision to investigate the *municipio*. Economic transformations can be brought about in various ways: An intrusive upper class can achieve local dominance in the framework of a colonial or semicolonial situation; rural regions can come under the influence of expanding urban-industrial sectors in such a manner that the countryside is brought within the orbit of dominance of urban influences, this being the typical modernization model. Change which owes little to alien influences is much less common.

Obviously, when we speak of "grass-roots" transformation versus externally inspired change, we are referring to relative influences. Zamora, as we have noted, is not an isolated enclave, but is now, and has been from the time of its foundation, articulated into the national culture. Still, the observation of one upper-class *zamorano* that "it is ourselves alone who have made Zamora what it is today," is essentially valid.

The observation, however, must still be set in the context of the times. It was because conditions were propitious that change was possible, which is not to say that it was inevitable. We have already examined what effect the Revolution had on the Porfirian pattern of social and economic organization. The Revolution dislodged those in control and made possible the play of new innovative forces, and as such it can be seen as a favorable event orchestrated beyond the confines of the *municipio*; some local individuals simply took advantage of the opportunities brought about by the Revolution, although initially the Revolution and its aftermath was seen as a time of troubles.

There can be little doubt that the rise of the new Zamora entrepreneurs had to await the breakdown of the established order, a phenomenon that students of economic and social change have identified as a precondition for major transformations in other countries and at other times. But there is also the question of the degree of breakdown—too little may be insufficient to allow for a major reordering of society; too much may so destroy the social fabric that reorganization and a search for new directions is unduly delayed.

We should note that during the period of civil strife the town of Zamora suffered very little physical damage, and that while it changed hands several times, it was never the scene of a major battle. In contrast, the surrounding countryside was for many years given over to the depredations of assorted armed groups, revolutionary and counterrevolutionary. It was in the countryside that battles were fought, crops were burned, and properties looted. As a result, the inhabitants of the *cabecera* enjoyed a degree of sanctuary and were far less effected by the events of the times than were rural dwellers. The difference between town and country should be judged not only in terms of physical damage, but also in terms of general security. Merchants and shopkeepers, and other members of the established middle class, certainly experienced difficult times, but there was little uprooting of people or crucial economic losses.

As might be expected, the *hacendados* suffered most; they had more to lose and their interests were more vulnerable. At the other end of the socioeconomic scale, *campesinos* were also caught up in the chaos and fighting and experienced hunger, maltreatment, and occasional loss of life, but since they had little in the way of land and other property, they were not so much targets of planned despoilment as unfortunate victims of war.

What most concerns us in this section is the effects of the Revolution on the group that in due course would become the new economic elite of the region. Although mainly of peasant origin, this was already an intermediate group somewhat distinct from the ordinary peasant farmer. Many had managed to establish themselves as merchants and storekeepers in their villages and hamlets. Their businesses were small and their wealth limited, but what they had achieved had been built up as a result of shrewdness and much hard work. One should not imagine that the road from peasantry to small-scale business was an easy one in the years before the Revolution. We know that some of these men had worked in the United States in order to put together small amounts of capital, while others had engaged in *arriero* commerce and various itinerant trades. What is very evident is that these were self-made men who were suddenly faced with the loss of all that they had striven for.

The armed bands of the Revolutionary period were often little better than guerrilla units living off the land. While the properties of the rich were prime targets, they were in no way averse to replenishing their supplies from village stores and requisitions from the peasants. A former village storekeeper describes in vivid detail the uncertainties of the period:

> You never knew on waking up what might take place that day. Life was like a game of cards, except that in this game you generally lost. A column would come into the village and the *jefe* would gather the people together and tell them that he "represented the government," or the "legitimate authority," or simply that he was part of a force commanded by a certain general. Every leader had some military title—there must have been more colonels than in all the Kaiser's army—and generally he spoke "for" someone or "in the name" of something. In this way, I think, they felt they had a right to rob the people, since in most cases the speeches and the introductions were quickly followed by demands.

The life histories of Zamora entrepreneurs contain many descriptions of what were often little more than bandit operations. The two following episodes, perhaps more dramatic than most, illustrate the kind of problems faced by small merchants during the Revolution.

> On May 9, 1918, three soldiers of a Revolutionary band, the advanced guard of a larger mounted force, attempted to rob the store. Together with my father and brother we fought off these intruders for a while, but we were soon forced to give ground and retreat into the neighboring hills when more soldiers appeared on the scene. From our hiding place we watched the raiders break into the store, loot it of its goods, and finally burn it to the ground.

> In the course of the Revolutionary fighting various opposing bands sent their sick and wounded to Don ——— for treatment. The leader of one of Pancho Villa's bands heard that "Doctor" ——— had been treating some wounded soldiers from a Carrancista detachment and moved into town to liquidate him. Finding that he had fled, the insurgent colonel proceeded to loot the home and store of a man who had only been practicing Christian charity. He performed this task so successfully that nothing was left worth salvaging.[1]

Having lost their properties and hence all reason for remaining in the exposed, anarchical countryside, both of the men in these stories fled to the relative safety of Zamora. They were not alone. Others seeking refuge in the *cabecera* counted themselves lucky to have saved their lives and highly fortunate if they also managed to take a few savings with them. Zamora, due to its size and location, was generally garrisoned with enough troops to resist the probes of small military units. But the surrounding countryside, which lacked such protection, could be terrorized for long periods by even numerically insignificant detachments.

On the whole, *zamoranos* were bystanders in the drama of the Revolution, but

---

[1] The speaker is describing the experience of his late brother, a man who had been apprenticed to an itinerant physician and had subsequently established himself as the "doctor"-pharmacist of the village.

what occurred in those turbulent years was destined to have a lasting impact. The refugees from the countryside came less by choice than by necessity, but once in the town they turned their attention to making the best of what was initially a bad thing.

EMERGENCE OF THE NEW ENTREPRENEURS

The Revolution displaced the old elite and introduced a new component in the life of the *cabecera*. The options open to this intrusive element were limited by a number of factors: education, cultural background, and previous experience. It was precisely those capable of operating in an essentially ambiguous and chaotic environment that stood to benefit most from the break-up of authority and the general uncertainty of the times. The established middle class was little prepared to act as agents of change. They were less traumatized by the Revolution than any other element in the community. Times might be difficult and trade poor, but the conditions were not so bad as to preclude weathering the storm by such tried and true methods as belt tightening and keeping low. Furthermore, the middle class was hardly an innovative group and as such it was not psychologically equipped to spearhead a movement of change. For the most part, the peasantry lacked the skills to do much more than survive another catastrophe, and survival has always been the peasant's strong card.

Yet, the conditions we have described were not without possibilities for advancement by those willing to make use of certain skills and abilities. For instance, there were frequent and severe shortages of everything from luxury items to ordinary staples, shortages that could not be met by the traditional sources of supply. Also, the multiplicity of printing press issues (all kinds of paper money circulated in the *municipio*) raised the value of "good money," in particular gold and silver currency. Many citizens, *hacendados* and others, were only too eager to exchange goods and property for liquid assets offering some measure of security. From what I have been told, Zamora during the Revolution functioned in much the same way as parts of Europe during World War II. It was not so much that articles were unavailable, but rather that they had to be purchased outside the system in "gray" or "black market" transactions. In situations of this kind, profits tend to be commensurate with the risks involved.

Out of the many who sought protection in Zamora, some were destined to become men of great wealth and influence. What distinguished them from the mass of refugees? Certainly not their initial financial resources. As a case in point, an uncle and a nephew founded a trading venture with some 1800 pesos salvaged from their rural businesses. Other beginnings were even more modest. After describing the misfortunes of his family, an informant goes on to relate how they moved to Zamora and started a new business:

> The family then moved to Zamora and established a general store with the 300 pesos they had brought with them from the village. The store stocked all kinds of merchandise, including tobacco. Since during the Revolution many commodities were in short supply due to poor communications and the uncertainty

of the times, the store began turning out its own hand-made cigarettes, partly in order to meet the demand for this item, but also in order to provide employment for members of the family.

We notice in this anecdote that the family began to turn out cigarettes in part out of economic need—to provide employment for family members—but that the decision to engage in this kind of business also reflected their judgment that a good market was available for the product. Not mentioned in this description is the fact that sometime later a family member was fortunate enough to learn that a freight car load of tobacco (I got the impression that it had been "abandoned") could be purchased for a very reasonable price. This understanding of regional needs and condition is a theme that crops up in a number of life histories. Thus, the nephew and uncle referred to earlier decided to concentrate on "trade dealing in wood and alcohol, items allowing a high profit on initial investment."

This willingness to take advantage of conditions peculiar to a time of troubles may be accounted for in terms of both situational and personality factors. One should remember that Zamora had its full complement of established merchants and that in order to make some sort of a living newcomers had little choice but to tap "unorthodox" sectors of the economy. Although initially these new entrepreneurs could count on only meagre financial resources, they did enjoy some less tangible advantages. These included a thorough knowledge of the region and a network of personal contacts built up in the course of previous trading and business activities. With such interpersonal linkages and associated background information, it was possible for the newcomers to gauge local conditions, the availability of supplies, the current safety of communications, and so forth, more quickly and more accurately than competitors with more restricted contacts and horizons.

Thus, the refugees generally enjoyed what might be termed a superior system of market intelligence. But it was their willingness to make use of this knowledge that turned a potential advantage into concrete results. Of course, to some degree necessity dictated options: A poor man cannot afford to be fastidious and must make do with whatever openings a given situation provides. Also, such an individual may be more willing to take risks than a solidly established businessman. I would hazard, though, that risk-taking of a certain kind, that is, within the context of the region, was also to some degree "built in" into the personality of these newcomers. Even before the Revolution they were an emerging group, although severely limited by a social structure that permitted them to operate only on the peripheries of the economy.

The move to the *cabecera* was the first step leading to a substantial transformation of the regional economy and a restructuring of class and power positions in the *municipio*. No doubt it was the relative safety of Zamora that first attracted people from outlying regions, but once the move had been made, certain advantages accrued to those operating out of the township. After conditions improved and an element of safety returned to the Mexican countryside, increasing use could be made of the road and rail networks linking the town to its natural hinterland. Also, the Revolution concentrated a particular kind of economic talent in one central location. The nature of this talent will be discussed in the next section.

INVESTMENT AND BUSINESS VALUES

The values of Zamora entrepreneurs and their limited educational and technological experience require that industrial enterprises be small and based on relatively
simple technology. The typical Zamora firm produces primary commodities that
do not call for highly sophisticated manufacturing techniques. The typical Zamora
entrepreneur is hardly a technological innovator, but rather, a successful imitator
of well-established techniques. There are one or two exceptions to this generaliza-
tion, but the men in question are not typical *zamoranos*, but individuals with some
industrial experience outside of the region.

Industrialization in Zamora is due to a combination of essentially ready-made
techniques of production, the market knowledge we have referred to earlier, and
the ability of businessmen (abetted by a depressed labor market) to plow back
profits. In part, the *ricos* have become rich by making every peso count. Profits
represent the chief investment source. Money from family and friends (sometimes
in the form of partnerships) also finds its way into businesses, but banks, government loans, and the like figure only slightly in the investment picture. Entrepreneurs
are quick to point out the virtues of saving and the disadvantages of relying
on outsiders:

> I have always been very careful in money matters. When I was building the
> business I used every *centavo* of profit for improvements and expansion. It is the
> only way, for you are never then dependent on other people.

Another *rico* observed that "banks and well-off individuals will never lend you
money when you are in real need of it, but once you are firmly established there is
no lack of eager partners, and then, of course, you can do without them."

This ability to save and the related suspicion of outsiders (who are viewed as
willing to profit from the efforts of others) is probably linked to the social background and previous experiences of the majority of entrepreneurs. Being predominantly of peasant extraction, it is not unexpected that these men harbor
suspicions of impersonal agencies, be they banks, government, or "big business,"
and dislike feeling dependent on others. For much the same reason, many Zamora
ricos are content with modest levels of personal comfort. It is a fact that one can
seldom identify a *rico* by outward manifestations of wealth. The best dressed men
in the *municipio* are middle-class professionals, while the newest cars are owned
by successful shopkeepers. With little exaggeration one might say that among the
ricos of Zamora conspicuous consumption is conspicuous by its absence.

If the economic behavior of Zamora entrepreneurs can in part be attributed to
what might loosely be called a "peasant mentality" which stresses frugality and
independence, it is also true that past experience has acted to reinforce such attitudes. At the time when most of these men established their businesses, reinvest-
ment of profits and the borrowing of capital from family or close associates was
virtually the only available funding for a new business or the expansion of one
already in being.

We have previously noted that Zamora entrepreneurs are convinced that big
business, and to some degree big politics, are detrimental to their interests. It is
a question of power and influence. Large corporations and important men have

wealth and contacts and the use of these resources assure them advantages and privileges with respect to such things as permits and contracts, credits and advantageous "deals." This is much more than just a fiction, for at the national level those in control are a relatively small group of politicians, important businessmen, top bureaucrats, and PRI leaders. Wealthy though they may be, the *ricos* of Zamora are not in this league and generally prefer not to play the economic game at the national level. However, if these *zamoranos* are more content being big fish in a small pond than small fish in a large one, it does not follow that their modes of operation vary greatly from that of their national competitors—other than in scale. Within their bailiwick, the *ricos* are men of consequence, a tight group of able manipulators not averse to using their power for economic gain and advantage.

Regional economic development has been favored by two features which affect the investment situation. One of these concerns the economic and social conditions of postrevolutionary Mexico; the second the nature of the local labor market. The circumstances we have outlined allowed the *ricos* to entrench themselves in the years following the Revolution. Economic dominance was further reinforced by the nature of the labor market. Zamora is currently, and has been for the full period of its industrial development, a region with a definite labor surplus. A labor surplus depresses wages and permits what may be termed "development on the cheap." It is also worth noting that since the "consolidation" of the Revolution—roughly the late 1930s—the Mexican economy has been gripped by inflationary pressures. In the country as a whole, price increases have consistently outstripped wage increases, a phenomenon which economists refer to as "stickiness of wages." Although we lack statistics on the local wage-price situation, the availability of excess labor in Zamora has no doubt worked to keep wages even lower in Zamora than in many other regions of Mexico. In the major industrial areas, such as Mexico City and Monterrey, the institutional power of the labor unions, which in Mexico as in many other developing countries, represents a kind of "aristocracy of the proletariat," has acted to keep the wages of union members more in line with rises in the standard of living. Unionization in Zamora, though, is virtually nonexistent and thus few pressures are placed on businessmen to increase the wages of their workers.

FAMILY AND FIRM IN ZAMORA

In Zamora, the control of a business enterprise is typically centralized in the hands of one man, the owner or the descendant of the owner, and transmitted on his death to a male next of kin, usually the owner's son. While alive, or at least in the possession of his faculties, the *patron*, boss or owner, exercises almost total discretion and responsibility over business affairs. To some extent, such a concentration of decision-making power is inevitable in a system that operates in a milieu of face-to-face relationships, for it is in the nature of such systems that every relationship must be viewed as a separate and distinct case to be dealt with according to its individual features rather than in the light of some general policy. Zamora businesses are structured around the family. This holds true for both the commercial enterprises of the long-established middle class and the industrial firms that have been founded in the course of the last thirty years. In agriculture as well, the Zamora ideal is also that of the family-run farm, although as population grows and pressures on the land increase, more *campesinos* are forced to look for work elsewhere, or at least to supplement their farm earnings with outside employment, including migrant labor.

In recent years, the thesis that industrialization leads to the break-up of extended kin ties has been seriously questioned by social scientists and economic historians. But whatever may have been the case in other locations or at other times, even a cursory examination of Zamora entrepreneurial history shows that industrialization (at least for those in control) has in fact reinforced family ties. The farmer's family may have to break-up when there is not enough land to support it, but the large businesses of the *cabecera* are of sufficient size to maintain large families.

The family-based business, though, is more than a system of family welfare or an instrument of entrepreneurial continuity. Given the undisputed control of the family head, a control which is reinforced by all the interlocking values of *mestizo* society, a business so organized assures the entrepreneur the services of a loyal and disciplined retinue. There is virtually no questioning of this authority by sons, nephews, and other junior family members. The son of an entrepreneur explained the situation quite cogently:

> You would be right to call this a family business, but do not forget that it was founded by one man, my father. My father is getting old now, and it may be that some of his ideas are not the most modern. Still, it was he who struggled, he who knew poverty and hard times. When asked for advice I give it gladly, and if I learn of something that will help the firm, I pass on the information. But I never forget that the final decisions rest with my father. The firm is my patrimony, but while my father lives he is the chief and I would not want it otherwise.

Such a system is not without its advantages, especially in a cultural environment—not Zamora alone—where standards of interpersonal ethics are not noticeably high. It is generally assumed in Zamora that greater reliance may be placed on one's kin than on outsiders. Perhaps nothing shows this clearer than a case where such ties were absent. In the course of an interview, I enquired of a certain entrepreneur about the duties performed by his assistant. After outlining some of the assistant's responsibilities, he commented: "Sr. _____ has been my *hombre de confianza* [a term meaning "man of trust"] for many years. I have absolute trust in him; he is like family."

The family-staffed firm may enjoy certain advantages, but a price must be paid for security and obedience. Quite obviously, when the chief criterion determining the allocation of important posts is kinship rather than competence (not that the two are mutually exclusive), quality can suffer. As in every kinship-based system, the operation of the family firm entails rights as well as obligations. Thus, family members often believe that kinship entitles them to special consideration—the closer the kinship the greater the consideration.

The entrepreneur can count on loyal subordinates (incidentally, I did not come across a single case of embezzlement or similar malpractice), but the other side of the coin is that the entrepreneur is expected to find a place in the firm for a great number of kinsmen. I received the distinct impression that many firms were overstaffed by family members holding down routine, and perhaps even superfluous, jobs. The monopoly of decision-making functions by the entrepreneur is a partial solution to the problem; individuals who do only hack work, or whose authority is severely circumscribed, are in no position to compromise the organization.

Such a concentration of responsibility may function satisfactorily for a time, but it does not make for a long-term solution. The family firm is by nature endogamous in that future management is typically recruited from within the family. But the greater the authority and the power of the entrepreneur, the fewer are the opportunities for initiative and responsibility by other members of the organization. The problem may not be acute during the directorship of owner-founders, but such authoritarian control can hardly provide an ideal training ground for those destined to direct the firm in future years.

The patterns of paternal dominance which we have referred to can in part be viewed as "functional"—they help to maintain the system and mitigate against authority and initiative being exercised by less-than-competent subordinates. However, it must be recognized that authoritarian control is something more than an attempt to develop a workable system; authoritarianism is part of a general culture pattern, and as such is not discretionary but operates regardless of the quality of subordinate personnel. We may say that it is a feature of the system rather than an attempt to consciously correct some of its shortcomings; in some degree, the "solution" is in part responsible for the "problem."

In Zamora, authoritarian control of business operations generally goes together with conservative business practices. A relatively stable market situation, in combination with the external "dangers" previously alluded to, has probably reduced the willingness of Zamora entrepreneurs to undertake the risks of expanding beyond the regional frame. Also, the near-monopoly which entrepreneurs enjoy within the region, and the relatively small numbers of productive units involved, have encouraged businessmen to minimize competition, control conditions of employment, and regularize the division of available markets.

Any evaluation of Zamora entrepreneurship must also take into account the fact that the firm operates both as a productive unit and as an extension of the family—that it fulfills multiple functions. This means that other than purely economic considerations are taken into consideration. Business is conceived not simply as a mechanism for the production and distribution of goods, but also as an enterprise that helps maintain the family and enhance its position in society. These goals are not unlike those of the peasant farmer, who in Mexico, as in many other lands, perceives his work as a means of livelihood for himself and his family, rather than a business run strictly for profit. Again, we have to bear in mind the social background of Zamora *ricos*.

THE ENTREPRENEUR AND SOCIETY

Every successful upwardly mobile group has had to cope with problems generated by its own success. The literature of industrialization and economic change shows that in the majority of cases the dynamics of ascendancy cannot be understood as a simple substitution of values, classes, and individuals. While a relatively small number of newly ascended individuals may greatly alter the composition of an elite, influences from established groups generally act to counter, neutralize, or coopt emergent groups.

We must understand this tendency towards assimilation from the vantage point of both the established group and the ascendant one. With regard to the former, it is an attempt to maintain influence, to survive by amalgamation. When it comes to the test, established elites usually prefer compromise to extinction. For their part, newly dominant groups are often extremely conscious of their cultural and social rawness.

Students of entrepreneurial history have remarked that under certain circumstances the influence of traditional upper strata on ascending groups is especially strong. This is so when on the one hand the traditional way of life manages to retain prestige and appeal, and on the other, some features characteristic of the rising group are stigmatized or disparaged.

We would not claim that European or American entrepreneurial history offers totally valid guidelines for events in postrevolutionary Zamora. We are not only dealing with a much more reduced frame, but a number of special considerations must be taken into account. To begin with, one of the consequences of the Revolution in Zamora was the withdrawal from the local scene of the old traditional aristocratic group, the *hacendados*. This exodus certainly aided the consolidation of power by the new *ricos*, but it also denied them a potential model for emulation. The local aristocracy, like most such classes, had a certain breadth of perspective. While it was in no sense a progressive group, it did contain a fair number of individuals who were at home not only in Zamora, but also in the great urban centers of Mexico, and in some instances, even abroad. What the old aristocracy could offer was not new ideas but a cosmopolitan orientation and a certain *savoir-faire*.

We have also noted that the bulk of Zamora entrepreneurs came from peasant backgrounds, not typical *campesinos* but still countrymen, a stratum of society traditionally looked down upon as gauche and uncouth. The zamora *ricos*, men with definite abilities and ambitions, would naturally attempt to remedy this image. We know that events conspired to provide the *ricos* with but one feasible group, the established middle class of the *cabecera*, to act the role of cultural and social mentors. That these "donors" were, and are, a very provincial and conservative class cannot be doubted. We may say that to the native conservatism of the *ricos*, there was grafted a new element, the small-town traditionalism of the *cabecera* bourgeoisie.

9 / Continuity and change

FIRST IMPRESSIONS

I returned to Zamora in the summer of 1971 after an absence of thirteen years. Unfortunately, my stay was short—about four weeks—but long enough, however, to appreciate that much had changed, but also that much had remained the same. Some of the changes were more obvious, others less so, but more fundamental.

The day of my arrival was a Sunday, the big market day in the *cabecera*, and as I had done on many a Sunday a dozen years earlier, I made my way to the municipal market to look at the vendors and customers, examine the products offered for sale, drink a beer at one of the many stalls catering to the hunger and thirst of *campesinos* and visiting Tarascan Indians; in short, watch *zamoranos* and the inhabitants of surrounding villages at their ease and engaging in their favorite pastime of buying and looking, selling and talking.

The first impression was one of sameness. The Tarascan women were still dressed in their long skirts and embroidered blouses, some moving through the stalls, others squatting on their heels in front of little batches of fruit or arrays of baskets. The *mestizo* peasants had not changed much either. There were the same family groups, always, it would seem, with a string of young children in tow. The same food was for sale—the mangoes, the sun-dried chili peppers, the strings of onions, the tortillas hot off the *comal*. And the hawkers were still crying their wares: "*Pantalones de contrabando*"—contraband trousers—"direct from Laredo, ten pesos while they last!" or, "You can now enjoy the benefits of medical science, I have a direct-from-the-factory shipment of the famous Dr. Alavarez pills, good for all manner of debilitating diseases!" Pills, one gathered, that would "clean the blood," restore potency, stimulate the liver, and counteract "female ailments." A few free samples wrapped in tissue paper were handed out to eager *campesinos*.

And yet, as one surveyed the scene more closely, some features, some elements, were not part of that older Zamora. The market has always had music, radios playing full blast, and on special occasions, live performers. I followed the crowd to a new concrete barn-like structure abutting the old municipal market to listen to the musicians and drink another beer (the price of admission). Long before I entered the enclosure, past a crowd of curious Indians from the *sierra*, it was evident that a new sound had been added to the traditional *mariachi* airs of *ranchero* music, which is the Mexican equivalent of "country and western." On a raised platform four young musicians and their electronic instruments were belting out the rock music of the seventies, and the lettering on the big drum proclaimed that we were listening to "Los Little Stones." Musicians with long hair and wire-rim dark glasses, beads and bell-bottoms, had come from the state capital to perform in Zamora. Even more surprising, the group included a booted and mini-skirted young woman going through all the appropriate gyrations—and much appreciated by the males in the audience for this reason. Most people were content to listen and drink their cokes and beers. Only a handful of customers danced, a young couple and two subteen girls.

I asked some young *campesinos* how long such performances had been given, and whether they were popular. Very popular among the young, I was told, and available for quite a while. In fact, Zamora even had its own group of amateur rock players. I left the performance after a few numbers, and close to the exit there was a vendor selling what he referred to as "hippy jewelry"; factory-made zodiac signs encased in clear plastic hanging from thin metal chains and big, multicolored, ceramic beads.

Other impressions of the first few days are perhaps not as vivid but significant nonetheless. New suburban developments to house a growing number of middle-income people as well as a new group of wealthy families; a Club Campestre, or country club, on the outskirts of the town; a modern hospital-infirmary erected by IMSS (Instituto Mexicano de Seguro Social), the social security agency; new stores and new factories; many more motor cars; and what can perhaps be described

New shopping and office complex nearing completion on outskirts of Zamora.

as a new cosmopolitanism. Zamora is no longer a small town but a bustling city with more than 50,000 inhabitants. In 1958, the trip from Mexico City to Zamora entailed not only distance but a definite shift from a metropolitan style of life to a provincial and simpler setting. The contemporary Zamora is not the national capital in microcosm, but the gap has narrowed, narrowed appreciably, especially for the comfortably well-off and the rich. This change is noticeable in many subtle ways. Zamora, bulwark of the Catholic faith, now has a Protestant church with a congregation, I was told, of some 200 adherents. No one, apparently, finds this very remarkable. Increasingly, the pastimes are those of the city rather than the country. Middle-class informants who previously would have taken their families for excursions in the country, perhaps on a visit to one of the local spas, now frequent the country club, or at least spend a weekend afternoon swimming in the big modern pool of a local motel. There are many more "strangers" in town, people from outside the region, drawn to Zamora by its industrial growth and the wealth of its agriculture. All these changes are more apparent in the middle and upper levels of society, but as we shall see, appearances are at times deceptive, and there is a component of continuity not only among the peasantry, but also in the upper echelons of Zamora society. The scale may change, but some forms and relationships endure.

SOME PREDICTIONS

One of the advantages of engaging in the anthropology of change is that the investigator can indulge in predictions and, if lucky, can later return to the scene of his studies and ascertain the accuracy of his prophesies. To some degree, all ethnography is a series of predictions about the behavior of classes of people in given social situations. When we say that middle-class male *zamoranos* evidence certain behavioral patterns in their dealings with members of the opposite sex, or that *campesinos* organize their economic activities in a particular way, it is taken for granted that these are generalizations based on informant-derived information; the anthropologist cannot be at all places at all times, and he assumes that there is a certain order in the universe, that all things being equal (or nearly so), the unknown will resemble the known, the whole will resemble the part. If, indeed, social relations are patterned and replicable, it is not necessary—it may even be wasteful of time and effort—to strive for more than a reasonable sample of social activity.

But the predictions which we will be considering in this section are of a somewhat different order. They involve projections in time and estimates of influence of factors that we had reason to expect would come into play as the result of changes within the Zamora society (for example, the death or retirement of the generation of entrepreneurial owner-founders) and the impingement of forces from without (for example, the growing impact of Mexican national culture).

Based on the work carried out in 1957–1958, I designated economies of the Zamora type as Intermediate Enclave Economies, or IEEs for short. I indicated

(Pi-Sunyer 1967: 172) that an IEE may be expected to evolve when the following conditions are met:

1. A traditionally oriented elite loses control over the political, social, and economic life of the region.

2. A potentially entrepreneurial group is for the first time able to exercise capacities which under previous conditions had remained masked.

3. The would-be entrepreneurial group places positive valuation on some forms of enterprise other than strictly traditional economic activities and/or when such traditional outlets are denied or greatly limited as a means of achieving wealth or prestige.

4. The tendency on the part of the entrepreneurial group to utilize a locally based network of interpersonal contacts and relationships places a bias in the direction of regional activity.

Economies of this type—and related social systems—might be expected to develop in localities not dominated by adjacent urban-industrial centers. The assumption is that economic dominance of such concentrations tends to inhibit the establishment of regionally based economies. Historically, periods following the collapse of long-established traditional economic and social systems, but prior to the erection of new centrally directed economies, appear to be especially propitious for the emergence of IEEs.

I hypothesized that economies of the kind found in the *municipio* were middle-range phenomena in the process of economic transformation. "The evidence," I wrote, "points to the transitory nature of such economies, to an increasing vulnerability to external and internal pressures and malfunctions" (Pi- Sunyer 1967: 173). More specifically, I pointed out that the Zamora economy had developed in a protective environment permitting some degree of isolation from direct competition, but that one should not assume that this privileged position could be perpetuated indefinitely:

> The general trend in Mexico . . . is for the hinterland to be ever more drawn into a market of national dimensions. Improvements in communications, the growing role of advertising in establishing nation-wide "images," all play their part in permitting customers an increased range of choice.

> This is only part of the problem. As the processes of manufacturing and marketing grow in complexity, regional industries increasingly find themselves at a disadvantage. It is not simply a question of funds for retooling, but also shortcomings in interpersonal relations and a lack of technical and scientific understanding sufficient to grasp the significance and applicability of new technological developments.
>
> (Pi-Sunyer 1967: 173)

I then turned to organizational factors:

> Where control of a business is primarily through inheritance, it is often difficult to assure the quality of succeeding managements. In Zamora the majority of enterprises are still directed by their founders, but sooner or later sons or other kin will have taken on the responsibilities of control and direction . . . the sons of Zamora entrepreneurs do not on the whole have the same qualities as their fathers. For one thing, the second generation has been given little opportunity

to exercise power and discretion and as a result tends to manifest a remarkable lack of initiative. Also, the sons, unlike their fathers, have grown up in a climate of security that places a premium on compliance rather than creativity.

(Pi-Sunyer 1967: 174)

I assumed, in short, that the Zamora regional economy was not built to last and that in due course it would be displaced or incorporated into a larger structure of national dimensions. I assumed that the peasantry, protected by the *ejido* tenure system, would continue relatively unchanged, although pressure on the land would force an increasing number of *campesinos* to look for work elsewhere, locally if jobs were made available, in more distant parts if they were not.

THE NEW ECONOMIC SCENE

How accurate did these predictions prove to be? I was right that changes were in the making, but somewhat off the mark with respect to the shape of things to come. The expectation was that Zamora would be increasingly drawn into the orbit of national life, economically, socially, and culturally. It is certainly true that today the outside world impinges more strongly on Zamora than it ever did before. But the major force, at least economically, is less national than international, less Mexican than North American.

The key to the current economic situation is to be found in the development of commercial farming, in particular the fantastic boom in strawberry growing, a crop which is virtually all (at least 80 percent) destined for the American market. Strawberries were already a cash crop in the late 1950s, but they were grown on nothing like the current scale. At that time there was not a single freezing plant in the *municipio*, and those strawberries which were not shipped fresh to Mexico City or sold in roadside stands were trucked to freezing plants outside the *municipio* and processed into pulp for jam. Some of this pulp did find its way to the United States, but the American market was relatively underdeveloped and profits from strawberry pulp are considerably lower than those realized from the sale of whole fruit and packaged cut strawberries in sugar syrup.

The dozen strawberry freezing plants of the region are an entirely new development. In the peak period during the harvest and the weeks following it (from December to June), thousands of workers are employed by the freezing plants to sort, wash, and package the crop. The capital investment for these *conjeladoras* runs into the millions of dollars and much of the capital is external, in considerable part from the United States, but some also from other regions of Mexico. Local capitalists have also invested in the strawberry business, either in freezers or by providing credit to farmers and *ejidatarios*, but it is Americans and *norteños*, Mexicans from the northern states of the Republic, who dominate the business.

The formal land tenure patterns in the *municipio* have not changed in the course of the last dozen years. *Ejidatarios* continue to exercise use rights over most of the farmland, but legal rights and control of the productive resources are two different things. During my initial stay in Zamora it was already clear that while *ejidatarios* and smallholders might work most of the land, they were tied into credit arrangements with rich *zamorano* merchants and money lenders that substantially restricted their options.

The small farmer and *ejidatario* were chronically short of credit, and it was those who provided the credit that in large part dictated the crops to be grown and arranged for their marketing. This system of patronage continues, but to it has been added a new corporate feudalism: The freezing plants and their agents make credit available on the condition that given strains are grown and that the crop is sold to them. It was not possible to ascertain how much agricultural credit is made available on these terms, but the story that four or five years ago a single American agent distributed over 100,000 pesos worth of credit in one week gives some idea of the scale.

For the typical *campesino* it is a case of new masters and old relationships. The vicissitudes of the American market represents the dominant economic variable. When the market is good, farmers can expect a decent profit, but when the market is glutted, as happened last year, hard times are in store. It is the small farmer who suffers most at such times. One *campesino*, when discussing the strawberry glut, told me the tragicomic story of how it had proved unprofitable to pick more than a portion of the crop and how the fields had then been opened to livestock:

> If you had been in the *municipio* at that time you would have witnessed an extraordinary sight. Imagine our donkeys eating strawberries for fodder, amusing perhaps, but also very sad, for much work and time, much money, goes into a strawberry crop.

THE OLD ENTREPRENEURS

The old entrepreneurs of this section are the *ricos*, or their successors, of a dozen years ago. Most, but not all, of the businesses remain intact. However, these enterprises no longer dominate the economy, although two or three *ricos* have substantially expanded their interests, either by cashing in on the strawberry boom or by extending the scope of their operations beyond the regional sphere.

By and large, though, this sector remains relatively static and still tied to regional horizons. The impression I received is one of growing conservatism and rigidity. This manifested itself most clearly in a new fear, a new anxiety, about the social and political future of the country. It is almost as if having come to power in troubled times, the now comfortably established *ricos* shudder at the storm signals going up all over Mexico.

Since 1968, the country has been troubled by a series of internal disturbances of some magnitude. During the 1968 Olympic Games, which were held in Mexico City, left-wing student demonstrations were put down with considerable bloodshed by the army and internal security forces. There have been more recent student strikes and demonstrations, and during the summer of 1971, during the period of my restudy, right-wing vigilante groups, the *halcones*, or "Falcons," attacked students and other dissidents in the streets of Mexico City. The recently elected president, Luis Echeverria, called for an investigation and dismissed some prominent officials linked to the *halcones*.

These events have not gone unnoticed in Zamora and a fairly common reaction on the part of the well-to-do has been a cry for "law and order." One informant went so far as to state that "student revolutionaries should be met with bullets: it is the only thing they understand." Others stressed that it was the function of the government to "provide stability" since without it "progress and economic advancement are impossible."

Zamora, of course, is very much at the periphery of such events, but there is certainly a feeling of uneasiness. Businessmen complain that "the unions are asking too much," although in truth the power of the unions in the *municipio* is quite limited, while some *pequeños propietarios* fear a new round of agrarian reform measures, although again these fears seem unfounded. Perhaps responses of this kind reflect the current troubles in Mexico, but it was hard to avoid the impression that even in Zamora a certain polarization of opinions was in the making. It is interesting to note that the government, which some years ago was not exactly an object of trust, is increasingly being looked upon as the protector of private property and the privileges of the rich.

THE NEW MIDDLE CLASS

A middle class is not new to Zamora, but until recently, and with the exception of government functionaries and a few of the managers employed by private industry, the middle class was local and traditional, provincial in orientation, and the chief link of continuity between the past and the present. It was a middle class of merchants and shopkeepers seasoned with a small group of professionals. It was in the middle class that one found the greatest degree of local pride and concern for past-binding local traditions. The middle class prided itself on its deep roots, its knowledge of regional history, and its concern for *cultura*. This element has not disappeared, but is today overshadowed by a new middle class which is much more nationally oriented, and, as its members would phrase it, much more "progressive." It is composed in part of locally recruited individuals, individuals who have attended high school in the *cabecera* or who have had some degree of professional and technical training in Mexico City, Guadalajara, or Morelia.

But the style setters are much less local people than outsiders. The fact of the matter is that the growth of the town, including the establishment of the freezing plants, generated a shortage of trained personnel that could only be met by outside recruitment. The 1970 census shows that more than 5000 of the inhabitants of the *municipio* were born in other localities. These are mostly poor people, workers and landless peasants, who have been drawn to Zamora in the expectation of employment opportunities. But there is also a sizable component, how large it is difficult to say, that can be thought of as representatives of the national middle class—professionals, technicians, supervisory and clerical personnel. There are also 163 individuals who give their place of birth as outside the Mexican republic. Most of these are middle-class people with special skills. Some are from Europe and some are from other Latin American countries. Even a number of Cuban refugees have found their way to Zamora.

As a group, this new middle class thinks differently and reacts differently from the established middle class. Its contacts with the outside world are quite extensive. Many have traveled widely and tend to compare Zamora rather unfavorably with other cities they have lived in. While the returned anthropologist is struck by the changes which have ensued in the course of the past dozen years, the new middle class regards the *municipio* as something of a backwater. It is a town that lacks "facilities": The streets are crowded and narrow, the stores are small and do not adequately cater to their tastes, there are complaints that the "culture is very provincial," by which is meant that few first-run movies are shown, few concerts are given, there are "no decent parks for the children," and the educational infrastructure is inadequate. As one informant complained:

> Here we live in a town of 50,000 inhabitants, but in reality it is like living in a *pueblo*. Apart from the day-to-day marketing, we have to buy almost everything in Guadalajara. The bookstores stock nothing but magazines, and if we want to buy a record or attend a theatrical performance it means a trip to the capital, or at least to Morelia or Guadalajara. Believe me, if it were not for the car we would really feel isolated.

Although they live in Zamora and make their living there, the members of the new middle class identify less with the town than with a style of life that is national rather than regional in scope. Many insist that they are only in Zamora "for the time being" and that they have no intention of becoming permanent residents.

Unlike the traditional Zamora elites—the *ricos* and the established middle class—the new middle class is much more consumption oriented. Many live in the new suburban developments which have sprung up on the outskirts of Zamora. Their houses are unabashedly "modern," modern in terms of architecture and in terms of furnishings, decorations, and appliances. There is a concern for comfort that was hardly evident in the houses of the well-to-do when I first visited Zamora. In truth, the American researcher soon feels right at home in such a setting: The same modern functional furniture, the same comingling of the sexes in social situations, the spreads and the crackers to accompany the bourbon or the gin and tonic before dinner. Even some of the same questions and the same conversation: "Tell me about the Black Panthers," "Did you read about the secret Pentagon documents?" (the Mexico City newspapers were then carrying reports of the court battle between the New York Times and the administration following the publication of the Pentagon Papers).

These are people with a keen interest in the outside world and often with a substantial knowledge of it. In the main, they have a better education than other *zamoranos* and believe strongly in "progress." In both national and local contexts, the new middle class is a privileged group, and some at least recognize that the mass of the people remain poor and ill-educated. However, they are optimistic about the future and believe that if they have managed to make it, others can also. With respect to attitudes, they share with the *ricos* of an earlier period a belief in the virtues of hard work, but together with this goes a recognition that diligence alone is not enough, but should be combined with knowledge and education. Since many are engaged in administrative and executive duties

Middle-income housing development being built in 1971. Houses are small but modern and customers are mainly officials, middle-range executives, and technicians. Note TV antennas.

Suburban housing for the new elite of Zamora (1971). The discontinuity with traditional housing is evident.

calling for technological and executive expertise, they may be thought of as essentially technocrats, and in fact they have some points of similarity with the *científicos* ("scientists") of the turn of the century, men who also believed that the welfare of the nation was best served by good administration and technologically competent leadership. My impression is that this middle class, which has been emerging in Mexico for some time, but is only now beginning to make an impact on Zamora, sees itself as a guardian generation, a generation with a mission. It is not without social conscience, but it does feel that a period of social stability is necessary for Mexico to emerge as a modern country. We may take as fairly typical the observation of one of its members:

> We are on the brink of becoming a modern nation. I see the Mexico of tomorrow as a land of industries and rational agricultural practices, a stable country where work is available for everyone, a country that can hold up its head with pride. In order to achieve this it is imperative that we have enlightened legislation, but we cannot afford social disintegration. Given a little time all our problems can be solved.

The new middle class is not so much an entrepreneurial as a managerial and administrative class, although, at least in Zamora, the division between entrepreneurs and administrators is by no means absolute. Business is a game that can be played at different levels. Thus an engineer employed by a freezing plant is likely to invest his savings in an agricultural venture and an official working in a government agency may moonlight as a part-time business executive.

In conversation and discussion the members of this class stress "rational" economic practices with the frame of reference being the national economy rather than the regional. As understood by them, rationality entails a free market situation, especially for exports to the United States, adequate credit facilities for agricultural and industrial expansion, and the elimination of bureaucratic red tape. These aims are not thought to be inconsistent with some degree of protection for national industries such as tariffs designed to keep Mexican products competitive with foreign goods.

The life style of the new middle class is an amalgam of Mexican and American models. As we have mentioned, it is materially rather similar to that of the business-oriented middle class of the United States. Obvious pride is taken in possessions, such as the suburban house and the automobile. Middle-class men are quite conscious of their appearance, and middle-class women even more so. There is a fair amount of visiting, families take vacations together (quite often to the United States, especially California), and substantial emphasis is placed on the education of children. Political questions are discussed, but as a subject, business dominates the conversation of the males. Women are expected to be intelligent and resourceful, although clearly subordinate. The ideal feminine image is that of the "good homemaker": a wife who will be a credit to her husband. Children are expected to excel at school. Girls are far less secluded than were the daughters of the *ricos* and the middle class in the late 1950s. A good match is an important goal for a girl, but she is not expected to be a passive background figure.

The material aspects of middle-class culture, even the uses to which physical arrangements (furniture, rooms, houses, and so forth) and objects are put, are referable to the penetration of that new cosmopolitanism which some have called the "age of mass consumption." We should understand, though, that in Zamora, and in Mexico in general, the products of modern industrial society, in particular expensive consumer durables, are enjoyed not by the masses, who generally cannot afford them, but by what is still a relatively small segment of the total population. As in much else, the Mexican dilemma is one of broadening the base of participation, making the "good life," materially defined, available to groups and classes who are still locked in poverty. It is the poor, however, who make the good life of the rich possible.

The *zamoranos* of the new middle class are not unaware of this problem, and its very presence makes for ambivalence and lack of firm purpose. Thus, it would probably be correct to categorize *zamoranos* of this class as believing in the virtues of the democratic process, and yet the opinion is current that the country is still not ripe for democracy—it is too complex for the poor and uneducated. In much the same way, one of the new businessmen will concede that the only criterion for success and advancement *should* be the talents and capacities of the individual, but that life being what it is, connections and influence continue to count for much. Since such linkages are scarce commodities available mostly to those already in positions of power—at least in contrast to the relative powerlessness of *campesinos* and other workers—it is very difficult for lower-class people to participate in such networks except at the very bottom of the patronage ladder. In some ways, therefore, the position of the classes and the relationship between members of different classes have remained relatively unchanged, notwithstanding the more "enlightened" attitudes of the new middle class.

As a group, the new middle class looks beyond the confines of Zamora. It is much more mobile, much less parochial, than either the *ricos* or the older established middle class of town merchants and local contractors. However, there remains a tendency to view business relations as an extension of interpersonal relations. Certainly, much effort goes into cultivating the right people, having the right connections, and mobilizing family and kin in the interests of personal advancement and economic success.

PEASANTS AND WORKERS

The life of the peasantry has changed but little. It is somewhat difficult to evaluate the changes in the standard of living that have taken place in the course of the past twelve years. I would say, though, that *ejidatarios* and private smallholders have improved their lot marginally. There seems to be more money around. Housing is better, diet is probably better, and *campesino* women now more typically cook with gas than was the case when I first visited Zamora. Many more houses have electricity, and nearly everyone has a radio. Life is still described as "hard," but less so than in the late 1950s. These changes, while appreciated, are not major. There is still not enough work to go around, and much of the work offered by the new freezing plants is of a nonpermanent nature. Life continues to be especially difficult for those who do not own land.

The statistics indicate that there are thousands of new jobs in the *municipio*, but in the main these are of a special kind. The owners and managers of freezing plants have learned to tap a docile sector of the labor supply: women. Most of the new labor force is made up of women and girls who are paid minimal wages for the duration of their employment. No doubt this employment helps the families and individuals in question, but there is little in the way of job security. The work is unskilled and there are always plenty of would-be employees waiting at the factory gates.

A genuine working class has still to evolve in Zamora. Unions are weak and workers have few rights. We might say that the conditions which allowed the Zamora entrepreneurs of a generation or more ago to develop industries on the cheap are still very much present. As one businessman phrased it, "In Zamora we don't have labor troubles since the labor supply far exceeds our current needs." The region has always had a labor excess and as new factories opened up, more and more people crowded into the *cabecera* and outlying hamlets. A development of recent years is the growth of very substandard housing in and around Zamora, small-scale shantytowns.

This is deplored by Zamora boosters and would-be town planners, but little is done to remedy the situation. In short, the new Zamora industrial boom has mainly benefited the rich or at least the comfortable well-to-do. The poor, with the exception of some *campesinos*, are not that much better off. The public schools have certainly not improved and are more overcrowded than ever. Medical facilities, it is true, are better than they were, although medical care is still expensive for the poor. As a case in point, few *campesino* or working-class women feel that they can afford medical attention at the time of the birth of their children, attention that would cost them about 200 pesos.

Viewed in the context of the region, the *campesinos* and workers of Zamora today occupy positions of economic and social subordination that are in most respects the same as those which they filled at the time of the original study. The hierarchy of power in the *municipio* has shifted, not perhaps drastically, but certainly appreciably, but these changes have effected those at the bottom only slightly. For the peasant, it is a case of new patrons, new men of influence, drawn from different classes, but following well established patterns of control. The new middle class may in its orientations be substantially less bound to the regional sphere—it counts friends and connections living throughout the republic and even in the United States—but to the extent that it makes its living in the Zamora region, it manipulates local human resources according to the old ties of personalistic patron-client relationships.

Today, as in the past, the key to understanding Zamora society lies in economic dominance. There are those with economic power and those without, and those without remain dependent and subordinate. At one time, in the 1930s and early 1940s, it appeared as if the peasantry might achieve some degree of economic independence. They were granted land, but land alone was far from enough to ensure economic self-sufficiency. There was never enough credit, the markets were controlled by nonpeasants, and genuine political power never devolved on the *campesinos*. As a revolutionary experiment, the land reform program helped to alleviate peasant misery and dampened peasant militance, but did little to alter power relations.

Consequently, the individual *ejidatarios* and *campesinos* of Zamora are still dependent on the good offices, the influence and the power, of key men in the region. It is through these patrons, who are referred to as such, that the peasant expects to better his life in small ways. If a peasant has a bright child who wishes to get an education, the patron is the man to turn to for finding a slot in the over-crowded local school system. If a family member is sick and needs medical attention, or money is needed to tide one over until the next harvest, the attempt is again made to mobilize the patronage relationship. The reciprocal aspect of such favors is a willingness to follow the advice of the patron, and especially to use the patron as the intermediary in all major economic transactions. No laws govern such be-havior, it is strictly a matter of established custom, but to do otherwise would spell ruin.

It is interesting to note that relative power positions remain the same in worker-manufacturer relationships. It is surely not by chance that the new industrial enterprises have recruited their labor force from what is surely the most docile and least sophisticated (in terms of labor-management relations) sector of the popu-lation. Women are new to industry, they have little previous work experience; few norms, other than federal minimum wage legislation, govern their employ-ment in Zamora. If anything, industrial workers, and in particular women workers, have less to bargain with than peasants. *Ejidatarios*, after all, have as assets not only their labor and skill as farmers, but also their small farms which in the aggregate constitute the bulk of the agricultural land of the *municipio*. A worker whose job is to wash or package strawberries has nothing to offer but a willing-ness to work a given number of hours a week.

It should come as no surprise, therefore, that the industrialization of Zamora has in no sense destroyed traditional relations, altered the position of the classes, or opened up new vistas for those at the bottom of the economic and social pyramid. It is industrialization without breakdown of the status quo. The several thousand Zamora industrial workers are somewhat in the same position as were the first generations of mill hands in North America and Western Europe at the beginning of the Industrial Revolution. In time, workers and working class organi-zations may develop a power base of their own, but at present, having and holding a job is the primary concern. One should also remember that with the termina-tion of the *bracero* arrangements between Mexico and the United States, workers and peasants no longer have the option of seeking work north of the border, although illegal border crossings are not uncommon.

THE FUTURE

What does the future hold in store for Zamora? Zamora is no longer a small town in a rather backward Mexican state. External influences are today felt more directly and more immediately than ever before, but for the mass of the people such influences manifest themselves in superficialities and slight changes in the contents of everyday living. What are considered to be minimal standards of living require more ready cash than was the case a dozen years ago, money for goods and services, for such things as electric light and better clothes, for bus fares and movie tickets. Even at the lowest levels of subsistence, the economy is becoming more dependent on cash.

It is possible that in years to come poor *zamoranos* will demand more than the superficialities of modern life, such as the opportunity to drink beer and Coca-Cola, own transistor radios, or cook meals with aluminum kitchen ware. There may arise a demand for major structural changes in the social order, but as of the moment, there is little evidence of this.

What cannot be doubted is that socially and economically Zamora is today more thoroughly integrated into the mainstream of Mexican national culture. Of course, this is especially true for the upper echelons of society, in particular the new middle class. Those in control see themselves as local representatives of a national elite; they think not only in local terms, but also in reference to the nation as a whole. I believe that these shifts are nonreversible and that a return to Zamora in a dozen years would find such trends accentuated.

New (1971) microwave telephone facility. Zamora is becoming increasingly integrated with the national culture.

The big question in Zamora, as is true in other parts of Mexico, is the degree of participation in these wider horizons, material participation as well as participation in terms of ideas and concepts. Must the poor always remain dependent and subordinate? Are "modernization" and "progress" concepts that find applicability to only the well-to-do sectors of society? How long will the *ejidatarios*, the landless *campesinos*, and the workers remain satisfied with only token changes? There is a broader question that warrants consideration. The region of Zamora is shifting from an essentially rural area to one that is becoming increasingly urban and industrial. The 1970 census figures indicate that this shift is already well underway. We can expect new factories, different industries, in the Zamora of tomorrow. It is doubtful whether a new industrial generation will for long remain satisfied with the slice of the pie that was their parents' portion. It is perhaps enough to note that not a few Mexican observers of the current scene—the problem, of course, is one that touches the whole country—see this problem of participation and allocation as the crucial question of the 1970s. Will the national (and local) leadership respond to social needs as they become manifest, or better still, move to meet such needs even before the subjects are fully aware of them?

All these are questions that face developing countries in many parts of the globe. Perhaps in Latin America especially, the modernization model has done little to change the condition of the poor. The present leadership in Mexico insists that it will not abandon or sacrifice the masses, but in truth the condition of the people has changed little in a generation. We can hope that the peasants of Zamora, the workers in the new factories, will in fact be given an opportunity to share in that good life that up to now has been the patrimony of a relatively select group. Time should tell, but there may not be too much time left, for dissatisfaction and lack of confidence in the established leadership is rife in the Mexico of 1971.

Glossary

acomodado: comfortably well-off person

aficionado: individual interested or involved in a sport or pastime

arriero: muleteer or operator of mule train. Earlier in the century *arrieros* often carried contraband.

bandolero: bandit or highwayman

barrio: neighborhood

barrios bajos: lower-class neighborhoods

bracero: agricultural laborer, term often applied to Mexican migrant workers employed in the United States

caballería: a colonial land grant of slightly over one hundred acres

cabecera: the administrative center (town or village) of a *municipio*

campesino: peasant or small farmer

capataz: work overseer on a large estate

carbonero: charcoal maker

comunidad agraria: "agrarian community," one of the corporate and cooperative farming units established as a result of the agrarian reform programs

conquistador: Spanish soldier-colonist

corrido: popular Mexican ballad

creyente: a religious believer, generally understood to mean a person who considers himself a Catholic

criollo: a person of Spanish cultural heritage born in the New World. In Mexico, the term usually designates the American-born upper class of colonial times.

cristero: member of militant counter-revolutionary Catholic movement

cristiano: Catholic, especially a devout one

cultura: culture in the sense of "being cultured" or "cultivated," hence, *inculto* and *sin cultura*, uncultured

don: honorific title usually applied to prominent upper-class individuals (fem.: doña)

ejidatario: peasant who works land made available to landless agriculturalists through the agrarian reform land redistribution program

ejido: (1) land worked by *ejidatario,* in Zamora about four hectares (a little under ten acres); (2) more generally, all the land granted to a group of peasants in a specific act of land redistribution. These holdings are theoretically organized as agrarian communities (see *comunidad agraria*).

fiestas patrias: national holidays

guerrillero: guerrilla fighter, from the Spanish *guerrilla,* "little war"

hacendado: a member of the prerevolutionary landowning class (see *hacienda*)

hacienda: large estate worked by peasant labor in serf-like relationship to landowner

hectare: standard metric unit of land measurement equal to 2.47 acres

111

hidalgo: term usually applied to a member of the Spanish lower aristocracy in early colonial times

hombría: manliness

indito: diminutive of *indio*, Indian. Used by non-Indians in a patronizing and paternalistic manner.

lluvias: the rains or the rainy season

macho: male (see *machismo*)

machismo: the quality of maleness associated with strength, virility, and patterned dominance over females

mano and *metate*: pestle and mortar, implements used for grinding corn in the making of *tortillas*

masa: corn dough

mayordomo: agent or manager of a large estate

mestizo: an individual who forms part of the Spanish-derived national culture (language; legal, political, religious, and other institutions). In Zamora, as is true of much of Mexico, the term has little currency and people identify as *mexicanos* (Mexicans).

mexicano: Mexican, popular usage in Zamora restricts it to non-Indian nationals

mexicanidad: the quality of being Mexican and identifying with the national culture and institutions

milpas: fields, often used in reference to corn fields

monte: steep and stony land with poor agricultural potential

municipio: smallest administrative unit in Mexico. The town of Zamora and surrounding communities comprise one such unit within the state of Michoacán (110 *municipios*).

novio(a): fiancé, more broadly, boyfriend or girlfriend

palacio municipal: town hall

parcela: small-holding received by a landless peasant during the agrarian reform program. Also can be used to designate any small agricultural property.

Partido Revolucionario Institucional (PRI): the "official" political party in Mexico

patron: boss or other powerful person

peninsulares: Spaniards

peña: loosely structured group of young men who join together for recreation and company

pequeñas propiedades: literally "small properties," the term is something of a euphemism used by Zamora landowners to refer to their estates

pobres: the poor

Porfirian: having to do with the era of General Porfirio Díaz, president and dictator of Mexico 1876–1911

presidente municipal: highest elective office in a *municipio*. The incumbent is the chief civil dignitary and performs functions somewhat like those of a mayor in the United States.

primera cuadra: elite residential area and location of major stores in Zamora

ranchero: cattleman, Mexican cowboy

rebozo: shawl worn by Mexican women

reconquista: period in Spanish history (711–1492) during which the primary theme was the reconquest of Spain from Moorish invaders

ricos: the rich

secretario municipal: municipal secretary, the chief administrative officer in a Mexican *municipio*. Officeholders are appointed by the state government and exercise very substantial power

santo: saint, and by extension, the day of a saint in the Catholic calendar from which an individual takes his name *temporal*:   land cultivated without irrigation or much natural moisture

tierra templada: land with a temperate climate. In the classification used in Mexico, Zamora falls within this category.

tierras de humedad: land that is relatively wet or humid for part of the year, generally close to rivers or lakes

tierras de riego: irrigated land

tortillas: flat and round cornbread, the chief staple in Mexico

urbanizaciones: modern housing developments

valiente: "brave one," protagonist of *corrido* ballads

vergüenza: modesty or shame, especially as a feminine attribute

zamorano: citizen or inhabitant of Zamora, and more specifically, an individual with a consciousness of the town's past

References

Adams, Richard M., 1956, "The Cultural Components of Central America," *American Anthropologist*, 58: 881–907.

Foster, George M., 1960, *Culture and Conquest: America's Spanish Heritage*. New York: Viking Fund Publications in Anthropology, No. 27.

Friedl, Ernestine, 1968, "Lagging Emulation in Post-Peasant Society. A Greek Case," in *Contributions to Mediterranean Sociology*, ed. by J.-G. Peristiany. Paris and the Hague: Mouton and Co.

Gillin, John, 1949, "Mestizo America," in *Most of the World*, ed. by Ralph Linton. New York: Columbia University Press.

Lewis, Oscar, 1959, *Five Families*. New York: Basic Books.

——, 1961, *The Children of Sanchez*. New York: Random House.

——, 1966, *La Vida*. New York: Random House.

——, 1970, *A Death in the Sanchez Family*. New York: Vintage Books.

Mendoza, Vicente T., 1954, *El corrido mexicano*. México, D. F.: Fondo de Cultura Económica.

Murray, Henry A., 1943, *Thematic Apperception Test Manual*. Cambridge, Mass.: Harvard University Press.

Nash, Manning, 1957, "The Multiple Society in Economic Development: Mexico and Guatemala," *American Anthropologist*, 59: 825–833.

Ortega y Gasset, 1948, *España invertebrada*. Madrid: Revista del Occidente.

Pi-Sunyer, Oriol, 1967, *Zamora: A Regional Economy in Mexico* Publ. 29. New Orleans: Middle American Research Institute, Tulane University.

Redfield, Robert, 1957, *The Primitive World and Its Transformations*. Ithaca, N. Y.: Cornell University Press.

Steward, Julian H., 1958, *The Theory of Culture Change*. Urbana: University of Illinois Press.

Wagley, Charles, and Marvin Harris, 1955, "A Typology of Latin American Subcultures," *American Anthropologist*, 57: 428–451.

Recommended reading

Beals, Ralph L., 1969, "The Tarascans," in *Ethnology*, pp. 725–773, Vol. 8, Part 2, of *Handbook of Middle American Indians*, ed. by Robert Wauchope and Evon Z. Vogt. Austin: University of Texas Press.
A recently published summary of anthropological studies on the Tarascan Indians. Good bibliography on the major sources for this population.

Cline, Howard F., 1962, *Mexico, from Revolution to Evolution*. Oxford: Oxford University Press.
A good account of recent Mexican history with emphasis on developments since the Revolution.

Diaz, May N., 1966, *Tonalá: Conservatism, Authority and Responsibility in a Mexican Town*. Berkeley and Los Angeles: University of California Press.
An ethnography of a Mestizo town near Guadalajara. Emphasis is on economic and social change and the penetration of big city influences on a previously traditional community.

Foster, George M., 1961, "The Dyadic Contract: A Model for the Social Structure of a Mexican Peasant Village," *American Anthropologist*, 63: 1173–1192.
A description and analysis of peasant social relations.

————, 1967, *Tzintzuntzan: Mexican Peasants in a Changing World*. Boston: Little, Brown and Company.
One of the best studies of peasant life in western Mexico.

Fromm, Erich, and Michael Maccoby, 1970, *Social Character in a Mexican Village*. Englewood Cliffs, N. J.: Prentice-Hall, Inc.
A study of the personality and culture of Mexican peasants. Much information on psychological testing and analysis.

Nash, Manning, 1957, "The Multiple Society in Economic Development: Mexico," *American Anthropologist*, 59: 825–833.
Economic and cultural change in the context of Mexican cultural pluralism.

Needler, Martin, C., 1971, "Politics and National Character: The Case of Mexico," *American Anthropologist*, 73: 757–761.
A study of Mexican "political culture" and the degree to which institutions at the national level reflect authority patterns in the wider culture.

Nelson, Cynthia, 1971, *The Waiting Village, Social Change in Rural Mexico*. Boston: Little, Brown and Company.
An excellent little ethnography of a Michoacán village. The author is primarily concerned with the relationships between personality, entrepreneurship, and economic change.

Paz, Octavio, 1971, *The Labyrinth of Solitude*, trans. by Lysander Kemp. New York: Grove Press, Inc.
A fascinating and incisive study of Mexican national character by a leading Mexican writer.

Pi-Sunyer, Oriol, 1967, *Zamora: A Regional Economy in Mexico*, Publ. 29. New Orleans: Middle American Research Institute, Tulane University.
Economic relationships in the Zamora region viewed in the framework of local and national culture.

Ramos, Samuel, 1962, *Profiles of Man and Culture in Mexico*, trans. by Peter G. Earle. Austin: University of Texas Press.
A pioneering work on the configurations of Mexican cultures and personality. First published almost forty years ago, this classic is recommended to all who wish to understand modern Mexico.

Simpson, Lesley Byrd, 1967, *Many Mexicos*, 4th rev. ed. Berkeley and Los Angeles: University of California Press.
Perhaps the best short history of Mexico available in the English language.

Wagley, Charles, and Marvin Harris, 1955, "A Typology of Latin American Subcultures," *American Anthropologist*, 57: 428–451.
Although not limited to Mexico, this analysis of the variety of Latin American culture types is most pertinent to an understanding of contemporary Mexican national culture, ethnic relations, and urban-rural differences.

West, Robert C., 1948, *Cultural Geography of the Modern Tarascan Area*, Publ. 7. Washington: Smithsonian Institution, Institute of Social Anthropology.
The standard reference on the habitat and environment of the Tarascan area. Since Indian and Mestizo communities are often juxtaposed, this monograph is hardly less useful to those mainly concerned with neighboring Spanish-speaking villages.

Whiteford, Andrew H., 1960, *Two Cities in Latin America: A Comparative Description of Social Classes*, Bull. 9. Beloit, Wisc.: Logan Museum of Anthropology.
One of the few anthropological studies of substantial Latin American provincial towns. The material on Queretaro shows some interesting points of comparison with data from Zamora.

Wolf, Eric R., 1956, "Aspects of Group Relations in a Complex Society: Mexico," *American Anthropologist*, 58: 1065–1078.
A study of the ties between communities and the larger national institutions. Material is drawn from Mexico, but the model of interdependence has applicability to other complex societies.

———, 1966, "Kinship, Friendship, and Patron-Client Relations in Complex Societies in *The Social Anthropology of Complex Societies*, ed. by Michael Benton. London: Tavistock Publications.
A discussion of various "broker" groups and mediating relationships in complex societies. Much of the case material is drawn from the author's Mexican experience.